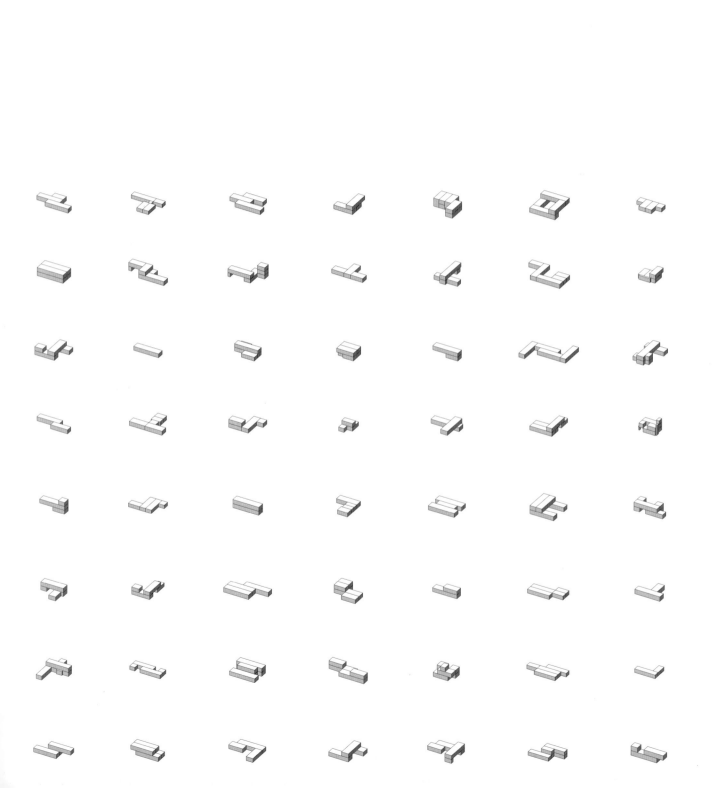

Princeton Architectural Press   New York

AUTHORS:
Joseph Tanney and Robert Luntz

FOREWORD:
Allison Arieff

MODERN MODULAR

The Prefab Houses of
RESOLUTION: 4 ARCHITECTURE

COPYRIGHT

Published by
Princeton Architectural Press
A McEvoy Group company
202 Warren Street
Hudson, New York 12534

Visit our website at www.papress.com.

Editors: Meredith Baber and Jacob Moore
Designer: Jan Haux

Special thanks to: Sara Bader, Nicola Bednarek
Brower, Janet Behning, Fannie Bushin, Megan
Carey, Carina Cha, Andrea Chlad, Barbara
Darko, Benjamin English, Russell Fernandez, Will
Foster, Jan Hartman, Diane Levinson, Jennifer
Lippert, Katharine Myers, Lauren Palmer,
Margaret Rogalski, Elana Schlenker, Rob Shaeffer,
Dan Simon, Andrew Stepanian, Sara Stemen,
Paul Wagner, and Joseph Weston of Princeton
Architectural Press —Kevin C. Lippert, publisher

Library of Congress Cataloging-in-Publication
Tanney, Joseph.
Modern modular : the prefab houses of
Resolution: 4 Architecture / Joseph Tanney and
Robert Luntz ; foreword by Allison Arieff. —
First edition.
191 pages : illustrations (some color) ; 23 cm
ISBN 978-1-61689-051-3 (pbk.)
1. Resolution: 4 Architecture (Firm)
2. Prefabricated houses—United States.
3. Architecture, Domestic—United States—
History—20th century. 4. Architecture,
Domestic—United States—History—21st
century. I. Luntz, Robert. II. Resolution:
4 Architecture (Firm) Works. Selections. III. Title.
NA737.R47A4 2013
728—dc23
                                2012048679

CONTENTS

FOREWORD

And We Shall Know Your Typology: Some Musings
on the Work of Resolution: 4 Architecture

Allison Arieff

If we eliminate from our hearts
and minds all dead concepts in
regards to the house, and look to
the question from a critical and
objective point of view, we shall
arrive at the "House Machine,"
the mass-production house,
healthy (and morally so, too) and
beautiful.

—Le Corbusier, 1919

When we first started seriously
to think about the prefabricated
home, everybody jumped to the
conclusion that it would lead to
monotony. I say it offers us a way
of building truly imaginative and
exciting homes.

—Richard Rogers, 1968

Forget cookie cutter. Think
cutting edge.

—*Money*, 2003

The paradigm-changing power of prefabrication has been evangelized—and then routinely dismissed—by each successive generation of the twentieth century. The oft-maligned, periodically celebrated building technique has been described, and perhaps rightfully so, as a series of noble failures. Yet prefab practitioners persist at either, depending on your perspective, tilting at windmills or revolutionizing home building. (I vote for the latter.)

And no wonder—broadly defined, prefab has inspired an extremely diverse cast of creators, both in manner and in method. Thomas Edison designed a system from concrete. Buckminster Fuller believed the world was ready for a round (and prefabricated) house. Airstream's Wally Byam saw the technology succeeding on wheels. Case Study modernist Craig Ellwood believed all homes would be bought in prefabricated form and designed accordingly. William Levitt, perhaps most famously, dreamt of, and actually built,

row after row of identical versions of his prefabricated vision in the eponymously named Levittown. Prefab even entered the realm of cinema when Buster Keaton played a newlywed trying to build a prefab house in the 1921 film, *One Week*.

But despite this jam-packed century of obsession, no one was really prepared for the prefab pyrotechnics that took place in the early 2000s—a time when prefab underwent an unforeseeable transformation in status. Once seen as cookie-cutter at best, and ready to be obliterated by any passing weather pattern at worst, prefab homes were all of a sudden featured not only on shelter magazine covers and as the subject of glossy monographs, but as "must-haves" in the *New York Times'* guide to entertaining. By 2004, the *Wall Street Journal* observed, "There are problems to solve [with prefabrication] but they no longer appear to be deal killers….the force of a gathering storm of architectural talent and imagination does seem to have the makings of a movement."

They were right. The mid-2000s saw an explosion of interest in prefab, not just on the part of the architects who'd been sketching typologies in relative obscurity, but by an increasingly design-savvy public who was feeling empowered to seek out housing that met its functional and aesthetic desires (and didn't just satisfy the return on investment requirements of master-planned-community developers).

Leading the pack was Resolution: 4 Architecture.

I don't remember the exact moment I saw RES4's meticulous grid of prefab typologies on its website, but it was as if I had discovered a treasure map—a mysterious guide to my future. As it turns out, given the events that followed, that's exactly what it was.

The short story of how RES4 came to be one of the leaders of modern prefab has its origins in an unabashed passion combined with just the right amount of naivete, which many people shared a decade ago. By that I mean that there was a group of people so engaged, so committed to the pursuit of prefab that they were brazenly undeterred by the formidable obstacles that were undeniably present (and in many ways, still are).

Prefab had experienced cyclical surges of interest throughout the twentieth century but had yet to find a strong foothold in the profession. As the 1990s were drawing to a close, the field of architecture generally tended to turn up its nose at mass production, believing that it diluted both form and aesthetics. The general public still considered prefab tacky and poorly constructed, as did the majority of those in charge of construction loans and mortgages. Existing prefab manufacturers—busy building developer homes, warehouses, and Holiday Inn Expresses nationwide—were baffled by the modern designs being presented to them, and few were willing to take on what they saw as fool's errands. As cofounder Joseph Tanney once explained to me, in 2004 as RES4 was beginning to interview factory administrators to build its designs, "It's a different language. It's as if we're speaking German and [the manufacturer] is speaking Italian and we're both learning French so we can communicate."

That enthusiastic naivete was certainly at play on the day in 2003 when I marched into the office of the publisher of Dwell magazine (where I was then editor in chief) and said, "Hey, why don't we have a prefab design competition?" Luckily, I had no idea what I was getting into, because if I had, the Dwell Home Design Invitational would have never happened. Sure, prefab would have still had another one of its oft-recurring moments of glory, but the story certainly would have played out much differently.

So, to back up a little: in 2002, I published *Prefab*, what I thought would be a serious but small book on the subject. Not long after, a venture capitalist—a previously unheard of occupation that had become ubiquitous around this time—somehow came across that book at a Barnes & Noble in North Carolina and called me at work in San Francisco to ask where he could get one of those houses in the book. Since *Prefab* consisted of some gorgeous, technologically sophisticated one-off constructions, but mostly a lot of intriguing albeit unbuilt projects, I told him, "you can't," which was a truly reasonable response at the time. Meanwhile, as I would soon discover, many architects around the world were quietly sketching out their own version of Koenig's Case Study #22. Most thought they were alone.

Tanney, too, has often told me how he felt that his firm's explorations were a singular pursuit, that he had no idea of the volume of work that was happening in the realm of prefab. The reason? Most of it existed in the form of slick websites and alluring axonometric drawings. But the number of actual built projects was negligible in the United States, although countries such as Japan and Sweden have long recognized the merits of automated building systems and have built housing units numbering in the thousands. I couldn't understand why this wasn't happening in the United States. Why were the dismal subdivisions quickly blanketing

the American landscape the norm? Why couldn't there be something better?

As I began to do research for the Dwell Home competition, RES4 set the standard. Our plan was to select a group of participants who had been meaningfully engaged with prefab for some time, and the thinking behind RES4's explorations demonstrated a commitment and complexity that went far beyond the dabbling of many of its peers. But enough smart and talented folks were giving them a run for their money—firms like Marmol Radziner, Wes Jones, Collins and Turner Architects, and the Office of Mobile Design, just to name a few—and soon we had a group of sixteen firms and the competition was off and running.

Before we knew it, in May of 2003, the Dwell Home client (that same man who'd rang me on the phone looking for a house) came to San Francisco to review the sixteen architectural models submitted by an international roster of architects. Walking around the scale models displayed on the editorial floor of *Dwell*'s

offices, he didn't take very long to make his decision. RES4's winning plan managed to push the design envelope while adhering to industrial designer Raymond Loewy's perfect maxim, "MAYA (Most Advanced, Yet Acceptable)." RES4's response to the competition brief—to conceive an affordable, well-designed prefab home for $200,000—was based on prefabricated modules that could be inexpensively produced in a factory environment, trucked to the site, and craned onto a concrete foundation that contained all of the house's mechanical systems. These easy-to-transport modules could be configured in any number of ways to create limitless home-design possibilities. RES4's winning design created a program specific to the clients—their needs and their site (which could not be said of all participating architects). Two intersecting "bars" formed the house: the communal areas were housed in the lower-level bar, while the private spaces were in the second-story volume. Special materials and features like cedar siding, bamboo flooring, aluminum-clad windows, and even a roof deck with a fireplace highlighted the customization potential of RES4's prefabrication.

When the winning home was unveiled at the International Contemporary Furniture Fair in the spring of 2004, an unexpected media frenzy ensued. Previously pedestrian, prefab was now big news: Tanney was profiled in the *Wall Street Journal* and the *New York Times*, and we both appeared on CNN—all to discuss prefab! I began to receive many more calls from venture capitalists who had cashed in (this was all happening at the height of the first dot-com boom) and were interested in starting prefab housing companies of their own. Prefab developments were proposed, luxury prefab resorts were built in tony locales like Napa Valley, and an endless array of small prefab cottages were presented to the public, each with a cute, media-savvy moniker. Prefab was no longer cookie-cutter. Prefab was cool. Lenders loosened their resistance. Some subdivisions altered their codes, covenants, and restrictions to allow for prefab

and manufactured homes. Many other architects and designers jumped on the prefab bandwagon. This is not to suggest that all those poorly constructed manufactured homes were no longer being built; indeed, master-planned communities full of them proliferated at an alarming rate, particularly in soon-to-be foreclosure capitals in states like Arizona, Florida, California, and Nevada.

For most, the prefab arc peaked around 2005 as the nation's housing market went bust. It wasn't only prefab proponents, but the profession of architecture in general that saw everything come to a screeching halt. Luckily RES4 weathered the storm far better than its peers. I believe strongly that this is the case because, for RES4, prefab was never a trend or a fad ("pretty fab"), but was simply the most creative and efficient way to realize their vision. Those early typologies were, and continue to be, some of the most elegant expressions of prefab's potential. Guided by those first configurations, RES4 has delivered a

dazzling array of homes in sites as diverse as Jamaica, Vermont, and Locust Point in the Bronx with equal aplomb. Though they've embraced production, they haven't sacrificed site-specificity. The module is, to paraphrase Paul Rudolph, their twenty-first-century brick—but it is an unusually flexible brick, able to create an impressive variety of configurations and to please a plethora of clients.

For RES4, prefab is not a gimmick but rather a tool in its already packed arsenal of good ideas. As Tanney puts it, "The Modern Modular is a system, an idea, a concept, a method of design—not a product to be purchased. It is a way in which we think about, and ultimately execute, the manifestation of a domestic space." For Tanney and his partner Robert Luntz, this is no passing fad; for them, Modern Modular is here to stay.

COMPONENTS OF DOMESTICITY

The majority of residential modular manufacturers in the United States use a standard width of twelve, fourteen, or sixteen feet, based on limitations determined by the Department of Transportation. Although

KITCHENS

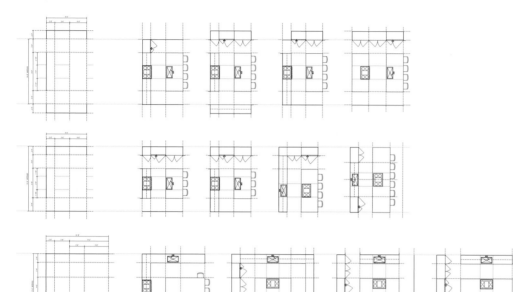

DINING

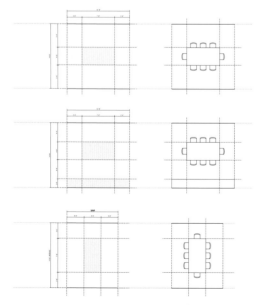

LIVING

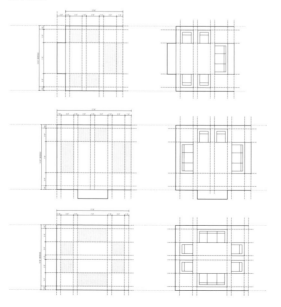

standard lengths of modules vary per factory, the most common is sixty feet, which is an optimum length in terms of filling assembly line space—the primary measurement of value in the assembly line methodology.

The essential elements of utility, such as furniture, fixtures, cabinets, and appliances, are broken down and reconfigured into basic components. These components are organized in multiple arrangements, based upon a dimension

that responds to functional requirements and efficiency of circulation. The results are compositional strategies that operate within a maximum width of sixteen feet, the Modern Modular's optimum dimension for domesticity.

BEDROOMS

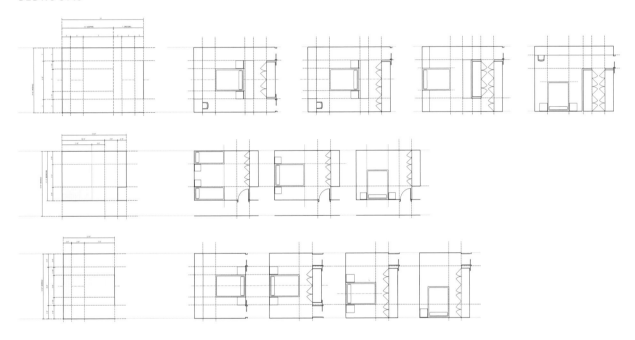

BATHROOMS

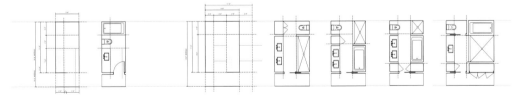

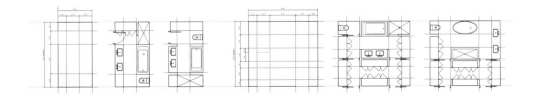

MODULES OF USE

Maintaining the maximum sixteen-foot width and sixty-foot length, the Components of Domesticity are arranged in contiguous relationships relative to use, creating linear bars we call Modules of Use. These modules are idealized volumes to be fabricated, conforming to the standard line space of the factory. Designed within the limits of the industry in terms of efficiency, both in use and implementation, these modules become the Conceptual Building Blocks of the Modern Modular.

COMMUNAL MODULES OF USE

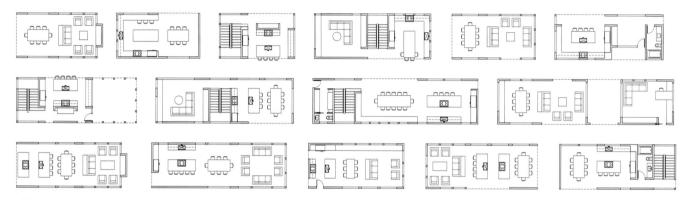

PRIVATE MODULES OF USE

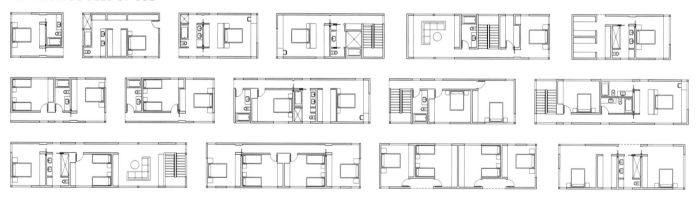

ACCESSORY MODULES

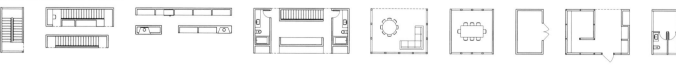

UNLIMITED PLAN VARIATIONS

Using the Modules of Use as Conceptual Building Blocks, an unlimited number of plans can be created in response to a client's specific program and site requirements. As a client's needs grow, so can the number of modules.

The plans are designed from the inside out: using the regulating lines developed within each component, elements are composed in relation to one another accordingly.

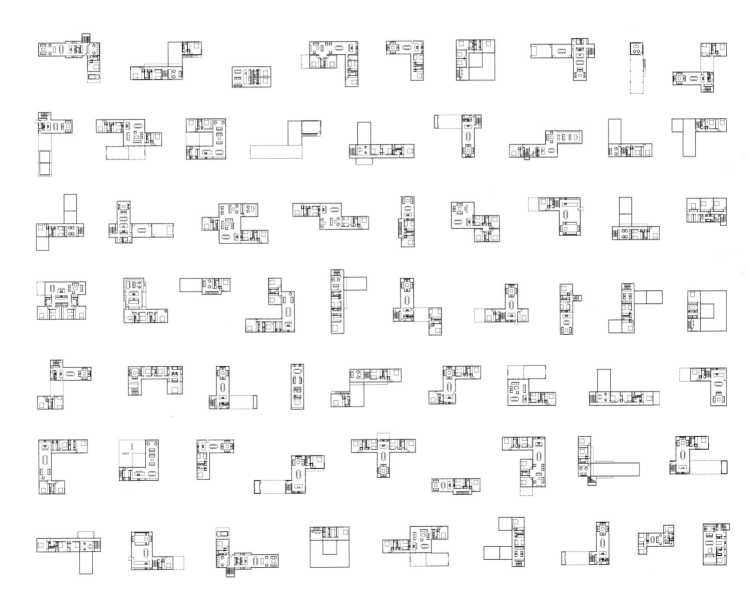

TYPOLOGY MATRIX

After a series of investigations, plan configurations began to evolve into seven basic forms, or types. Each of these types is thought of as a series, capable of expanding and contracting as needed, into one- and two-story compositions.

When the seven basic types are arranged horizontally, and potential sizes are organized vertically, a matrix of possibilities emerges. Analogous to Le Corbusier's Panel Exercise based on *The Modulor* and the golden section,

	1 MODULE 1000 SQ. FT	1.5 MODULES 1500 SQ. FT	2 MODULES (2 FULL LINE SPACES) 2000 SQ. FT				2.5 MODULES 2500 SQ. FT			
SINGLE-WIDE SERIES										
DOUBLE-WIDE SERIES										
T SERIES										
L SERIES										
COURTYARD SERIES										
TRIPLE-WIDE SERIES										
Z SERIES										

this volumetric exercise is also limitless in combinations.

The resultant typologies are concepts representing the potential of the Modern Modular. The intention was to create a process of design that operates within the limits of the modular industry, creating a higher degree of predictability of time and construction costs, while offering an opportunity for mass customization. Ultimately, the Modern Modular is a design and execution methodology focused on the efficiency of use and implementation, attempting to leverage existing methods of residential prefabrication.

3 MODULES (3 FULL LINE SPACES) 3000 SQ. FT	3.5 MODULES 3500 SQ. FT	4 MODULES (4 FULL LINE SPACES) 4000 SQ. FT

INTRODUCTION

Developing the Modern Modular

By Resolution: 4 Architecture—
Joseph Tanney and Robert Luntz

Although the single-family home has historically been a focal point in the exploration of architectural ideas, most people do not live in a space designed by an architect. As a small architectural practice in New York City whose work has consisted largely of urban residential projects, Resolution: 4 Architecture's focus has historically been the design of highly efficient, cost-effective, idea-driven spaces. Combining this experience of efficient urban domestic-planning strategies with our interest in off-the-shelf products and factory-based construction processes, we have developed a strategy for the mass customization of the single-family home.

Our concept, the Modern Modular, is a systematic methodology of design that attempts to leverage existing methods of prefabrication to produce custom modern homes, specific to each client and site. It is based on Conceptual Building Blocks we call Modules of Use. These modules have been derived predominantly from our urban residential work, which attempts not only to accommodate, but also to articulate and organize the essential elements of utility in contemporary domestic life. Our explorations have resulted in a series of freestanding domestic typologies that embody this essence of utility. The projects in this book represent a series of experiments to test this concept. The Modern Modular is a method of design—a theory really—with its roots reaching beyond the history of just our office.

During the latter half of the nineties, the United States experienced a rise in its collective design consciousness, specifically in terms of accessibility to modern design. With the introduction of *Dwell* in 2000, for the first time a magazine was completely devoted to modern domestic space, making modernism more accessible by shining a bright light on the lifestyles of regular people living in such spaces. Simultaneously, stores such as Design Within Reach, Target, and IKEA were making both high-end and everyday modern design accessible and often much more affordable than it had ever been before.

Conversely, residential architecture has been stagnant in its development.

Now a common point of discussion, the oversized and inefficient nature of most American suburban homes is an unfortunate reality. Americans are living in the past, with the country's current stock of single-family houses often representing a nostalgic image of what a "home" should look like, as opposed to being reflective of our domestic evolution. Although our lives are being modernized through access to technology, consumer products, and high-end appliances, the actual spaces in which we live have been slow to change—in terms of both their design and their execution. The fact that 96 percent of domestic spaces in this country have been built without the involvement of an architect is obvious. After all, designer consumer goods are mass-produced and relatively low-cost, but architect-designed domestic spaces are still individually produced and expensive.

Our speculation was that if we, as architects, could design a relatively affordable domestic space, we might be able to not only tap into the country's emerging and broadening design consciousness—a market that we felt was hungry for well-designed modern homes—but also effect lasting change in the American residential landscape. Of course, we weren't the first architects to consider using mass-production techniques to manufacture single-family homes.

Predating our exploration by decades, off-site production is often referred to as prefabrication or "prefab." Almost every home uses some level of prefabrication, though the prefabricated components are usually much smaller than the scale of the entire building. For the past fifty to eighty years, many architects before us have pursued this Holy Grail of modernism. Le Corbusier, Walter Gropius, Buckminster Fuller, and Frank Lloyd Wright are just a few who have attempted to design a relatively affordable modern home that could be mass-produced. In addition, several commercial institutions, such as Lustron and Sears Roebuck and Company, have also participated in the pursuit. Both

the more academic and more commercial paths have ended with varying degrees of success.

The numerous academic attempts were generally conceived as products with a high level of design, but were burdened with having to invent a complicated manufacturing process. Conversely, although the more commercial attempts achieved higher degrees of success in terms of efficient and integrated manufacturing processes, they were limited in terms of their homes' design flexibility—seemingly strangled by the process of production.

Rather than invent a new manufacturing process, our research focused on existing commercial methods of residential prefabrication. As they are currently employed by successful factories that are building homes everyday, the processes fall into three basic tiers, or delivery methods. At the low end of the spectrum, in both cost and quality, is the "manufactured home," which falls under the Department of Housing and Urban Development guidelines and offers very little flexibility in

design and product substitutions. At the high end of the spectrum is the panelized, or kit-of-parts, method of delivery, which offers the greatest design flexibility, yet often costs as much as building a house directly on its site. In the middle of the spectrum is the modular industry, which was born out of the manufactured home industry, yet adheres to all local codes and offers some design flexibility when operating within the industry limits.

It is with these regulations, determined by the Department of Transportation as the physical limits of what's allowed to be shipped down the highway (sixteen-foot-wide, eleven-foot-tall, and approximately sixty-foot-long modules), that we felt a kindred spirit. As a small firm in New York City, with much of our work having been the renovation of long linear loft spaces, thinking *inside* the box was a natural extension of our practice.

(See **Components of Domesticity**, pp. 12–13.)

Based on this experience, we began to design Conceptual Building Blocks that worked within the existing constraints of the modular industry. (See **Modules of Use**, p. 14.) We created communal Modules of Use containing kitchen, dining, and living areas, as well as private ones containing bedrooms and bathrooms. Then, combining these we began to develop a range of customizable typologies. (See **Unlimited Plan Variations**, p. 15.) The basic type became a Single Bar, with all of the essential elements of domesticity contained within a single module. (See **Typology Matrix**, pp. 16–17.) As the program expanded, we simply combined multiple boxes. We created Double-Wides, L's, Z's, and other variations that could be manipulated in an endless number of ways based upon site, orientation, views, program, and the many other factors that affect the layout of a home. (See **Developed Typologies**, pp. 21–25.) With little else, we posted a website and quickly began to get hits from potential clients.

With interest building, and since the typologies were, in truth, only *ideas* for potential homes, we decided to develop four actual case studies: Beach House, Suburban, Summer Retreat, and the Dwell Home. Intending to show more fully the potential of the original idea, we began to think beyond the diagrammatic typologies in very real terms, considering materials, details, and the manufacturing process. These case studies proved to be an important step in testing the Modern Modular hypothesis. (See **Case Studies,** pp. 26–27.)

Beginning with the Summer Retreat and the Dwell Home, we have now designed and built dozens of homes throughout the United States using the Modern Modular methodology, and are continually testing it with new projects. With each, we attempt to make small advances in the details, products, and technologies we employ. Of course, energy efficiency and sustainable innovations are central to every project. All of our homes are designed to meet LEED standards, and we have used solar energy as well as geothermal systems in many of our designs, so that they ultimately produce more energy than they consume. These technologies are becoming more and more accessible for the single-family home, and we have been consistently impressed with our clients' levels of interest in creating efficient and sustainable living environments—going further against the grain of today's typical residential development.

So far, this experience has validated our belief that a cost-effective modern option for the housing market has truly widespread appeal, and it is this kind of large-scale impact we aspire to have on national domestic design. In addition to private clients requesting individual homes, large multifamily developers and even entire communities have expressed interest in the Modern Modular. We continue to pursue and develop these opportunities. By becoming intimately involved with not only the design, but also the production of homes that are attainable by a larger segment of the population than has typically been able to employ an architect, we can have a much greater impact on our built environment and the role of our profession in shaping it.

DEVELOPED TYPOLOGIES

STANDARD BAR
870 SQ. FT

First Floor

A Living
B Dining
C Kitchen
D Bedroom (2)
E Bath

TWO-STORY BAR
1,430 SQ. FT

First Floor

A Living
B Dining
C Kitchen
D Bedroom (2)
E Bath

Second Floor

D Bedroom
E Bath
F Media Room
G Outdoor Terrace

LIFTED BAR
1,090 SQ. FT

First Floor

F Home Office

Second Floor

A Living
B Dining
C Kitchen
D Bedroom (2)
E Bath

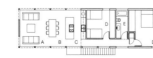

TWO-BAR BRIDGE WITH SLEEPING PORCH
1,960 SQ. FT

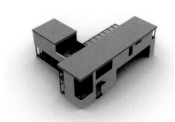

First Floor

A Living
B Dining
C Kitchen
E Bath
H Carport
I Storage

Second Floor

D Bedroom (2)
E Bath
F Media Room
G Outdoor Terrace
J Sleeping Porch

TWO-BAR L
1,790 SQ. FT

First Floor

A Living
B Dining
C Kitchen
D Bedroom
E Bath

Second Floor

D Bedroom (2)
E Bath
F Media Room
G Outdoor Terrace

TWO-STORY BAR WITH TERRACE
1,940 SQ. FT

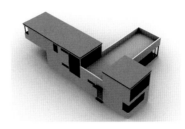

First Floor

A Living
B Dining
C Kitchen
D Bedroom (2)
E Bath

Second Floor

D Bedroom (2)
E Bath
F Outdoor Terrace (2)
G Sleeping Porch

TWO-BAR RETREAT
1,960 SQ. FT

First Floor

A Living
B Dining
C Kitchen
E Bath
H Carport
I Workspace

Second Floor

D Bedroom (2)
E Bath (2)
F Media Room
G Outdoor Terrace

TWO-BAR BRIDGE
1,868 SQ. FT

First Floor

A Living
B Dining
C Kitchen
E Bath
H Carport
I Storage

Second Floor

D Bedroom (2)
E Bath
F Media Room
G Outdoor Terrace

TWO-BAR SLIP
1,790 SQ. FT

First Floor

A Living
B Dining
C Kitchen
D Bedroom (4)
E Bath (2)

THREE-BAR SADDLEBAG
1,730 SQ. FT

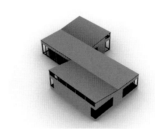

First Floor

A Living
B Dining
C Kitchen
D Bedroom (4)
E Bath (2)

THREE-BAR SLIP
1,980 SQ. FT

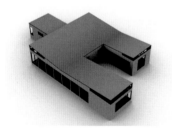

First Floor

A Living
B Dining
C Kitchen
D Bedroom (3)
E Bath (2)
F Screened Porch
G Open Porch

THREE-BAR T
1,575 SQ. FT

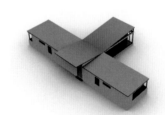

First Floor

A Living
B Dining
C Kitchen
D Bedroom (4)
E Bath (2)

THREE-BAR DUPLEX
2,130 SQ. FT

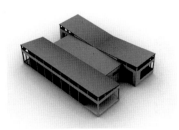

First Floor

A Living
B Dining
C Kitchen
D Bedroom (4)
E Bath (2)
F Open Porch

THREE-BAR PINWHEEL
1,930 SQ. FT

First Floor

A Living
B Dining
C Kitchen
D Bedroom (4)
E Bath (2)

THREE-BAR BRIDGE WITH GUEST HOUSE
2,660 SQ. FT

First Floor

A Living
B Dining
C Kitchen
D Bedroom (2)
E Bath (2)

Second Floor

D Bedroom (2)
E Bath
F Media Room
G Sleeping Porch
H Outdoor Terrace (2)

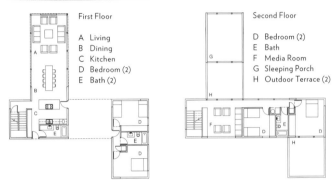

THREE-BAR BRIDGE WITH THREE-STORY TOWER
2,530 SQ. FT

First Floor

A Living
B Dining
C Kitchen
D Bedroom (2)
E Bath (2)

Second Floor

D Bedroom (2)
E Bath (2)
F Media Room
G Outdoor Terrace

CASE STUDIES

BEACH HOUSE

This two-bedroom, one-bath holiday home was developed from the Lifted Bar type. It sits on piers above the flood plane, with the Single Bar module featuring a glass facade and a wraparound deck.

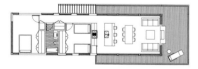

SUBURBAN

This three-bedroom, two-bath starter home was developed from the Two-Story Bar. A panelized saddlebag accommodates entry, vertical circulation, and built-in cabinets, while defining a parking zone with a trellis and garden storage.

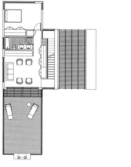 

SUMMER RETREAT

This four-bedroom, two-and-a-half-bath home was developed from the Three-Bar Bridge with Sleeping Porch. It features an arrival court with a private terrace and pool, and a screened porch that connects the wing to the main space.

DWELL HOME

This three-bedroom, three-and-a-half-bath home is a modified Two-Bar Bridge sited on a sloping lot. A butterfly roof module provides additional ceiling height with clerestory windows, collects rainwater, and is pitched for solar panels.

TYPOLOGY:
L Series Two-Bar Bridge

MODULES:
5 Boxes and Butterfly Roof

THE DWELL HOME

Pittsboro, North Carolina
2004

Prior to the 2003 Dwell Home Design Invitational, it was rare that a competition was held to design an actual home on a specific site, with a real budget for a dedicated client. Since it wasn't a purely conceptual domestic design competition, as is common in architecture discourse, the constraints required a comprehensive design methodology that would consider the process at every step, and control costs while maintaining a high level of quality. The winning entry is the result of the Modern Modular concept, and it became the first in a long and diverse list of projects built according to the method.

The Dwell Home is conceived simply as two bars: one containing private spaces, such as bedrooms and bathrooms, and another with more communal ones, such as kitchen, dining, and living areas. The bars are stacked perpendicular to one another to form an L. The lower, public volume is wrapped with glass and cement board panels, creating a roof deck above, while the upper, more private volume is clad in cedar and creates a carport below. The open office upstairs easily converts to a bedroom if required, and the storage volume adjacent to the carport downstairs can become a detached office—programmatic elements requested by the clients, a young couple planning for parenthood who both work from home.

As with all RES4 prefabs based on the Modern Modular, the Dwell Home was designed specifically for its site and the needs of the individual client. Yet, many of the ideas embraced and deployed here can be found in subsequent projects: the freestanding loft, framed space, kitchen as command center, kitchen/bath core volume, house as threshold, exterior–interior connection, abundance of natural light, clarity of public versus private use, high-efficiency HVAC systems, high-performance windows, low-flow fixtures, et cetera. With approximately 80 percent of this house built in a factory—and similar percentages in subsequent Modern Modular projects—the time required for on-site crews has been significantly reduced, minimizing the environmental impact on the local ecosystem, the waste discarded on or near the site, and the cost of transporting crews and materials.

After a steep and winding drive through seven wooded acres, visitors to the Dwell Home are met with a large opening in the south facade, a visual and physical invitation not only to the house, but also to the dense Appalachian forest beyond. With its simple, efficient, and powerful legibility, this portal—another feature often reimagined for subsequent projects—has served for our office as an invitation to future designs using the language of the Modern Modular.

Southwest corner at dusk

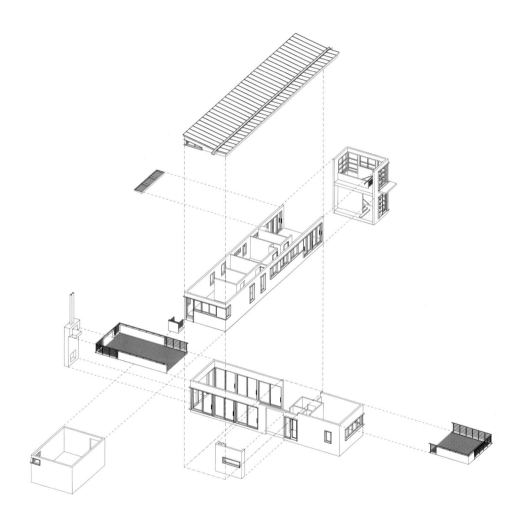

View from the kitchen island. The communal space is conceived as a freestanding loft, wrapped with floor-to-ceiling glass.

The interior space expands visually and physically to the outdoors via floor-to-ceiling windows, sliding glass doors, and connecting decks.

Located at the intersection of the two overlapping bars, the kitchen is the plan generator and focal point of twenty-first-century domesticity.

BOTTOM: A simple axis organizes the communal space, from the kitchen range to the fireplace, with a bathroom core located behind the kitchen.

View from beneath the portal showing the public deck that flanks the communal space and the private deck above.

OPPOSITE: The two-story volume of the house contains mostly private spaces and is clad in cedar siding with cement board accents, while the one-story volume contains public spaces and is clad in cement board panels with accents of cedar.

The Dwell Home under
construction in the factory.

BOTTOM: Roof module
being set, day two of on-site
construction.

Day four of the factory process,
showing the east elevation
of the second-floor module
containing stair and office.

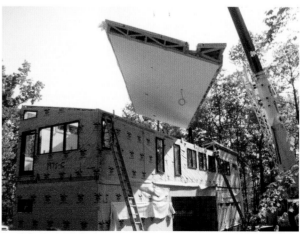

A   ENTRY
B   KITCHEN
C   DINING
D   LIVING
E   BATH
F   BEDROOM
G   DECK
H   CARPORT
I   STORAGE
J   OFFICE
K   MASTER BEDROOM

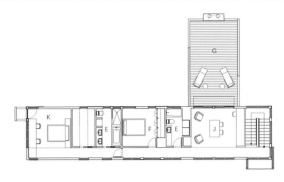

Second floor

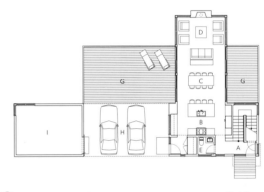

   16 FT

First floor

West elevation

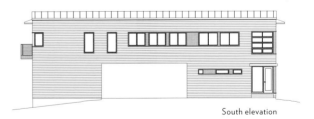

South elevation

East elevation

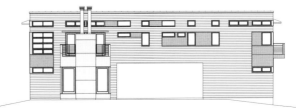

North elevation

TYPOLOGY:
Two-Story Double-Wide

MODULES:
4 Boxes

CAPE HOUSE

Eastham, Massachusetts
2006

Located in a residential neighborhood in Cape Cod, this home is a modern reinterpretation of the classic New England Cape house in all possible senses. Designed for a young family of four to supplement their primary residence in Boston, the new four-module home replaces a dilapidated beach bungalow—utilizing the existing twenty-eight-foot-by-fifty-foot foundation to expedite the construction process and save costs.

This compact, two-story design has a corner carved out to break up the volume and designate the house's main entry. The open communal space spans from front to back, leveraging the full twenty-eight-foot width of the double-wide module configuration. To further expand the programmatic needs of the client and speak to the site's vernacular history, a cedar-framed screened porch provides additional outdoor living space without modifying the existing foundation. Exterior walls are clad in cedar-shake siding commonly found on the Cape, further merging traditional and modern elements.

The home takes advantage of its proximity to the Salt Pond Bay with several outdoor terraces and a roof deck. An exterior fireplace creates an intimate zone for relaxation, even on winter evenings, with commanding views of the bay and ocean. The second floor contains the family's private spaces. A continuous stair from the basement to the roof provides easy access for entertaining. Upstairs and down, the house's window placement takes full advantage of summer breezes for efficient cooling, making it a truly year-round retreat.

Entry view

The street elevation shows how the new modular home sits on the preexisting foundation.

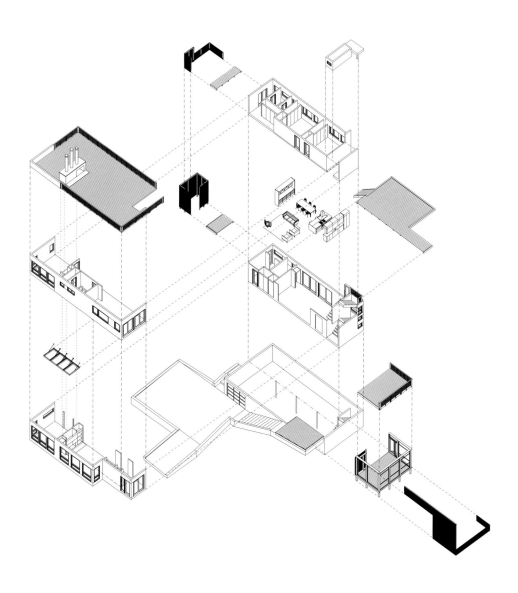

View of the dining room and kitchen with screened porch access beyond.

OPPOSITE: The living and dining spaces are created by placing two modules side by side. The first-floor master suite is located behind the fireplace volume. The edge is released for circulation, allowing maximum light and views at the perimeter.

BOTTOM: Second-floor master suite with fireplace and views to the bay.

The two-by-two cedar slat screen wall provides shade and privacy from the street while allowing views out.

Roof deck with views of the Atlantic Ocean.

BOTTOM: The exterior fireplace volume demarcates an intimate seating area.

Cedar-shake siding and white windows respond to the neighborhood's traditional Cape Cod vernacular.

BOTTOM: Two modules will sit side by side on this mate-line, supported by columns below. The exposed framing is temporary, used as shoring during transportation and setting.

Living room module being set upon the existing foundation.

BELOW: After being fabricated in the factory, the modules are transported to the site by truck.

A ENTRY PORCH
B KITCHEN
C DINING
D LIVING
E BATH
F BEDROOM
G DECK
H OUTDOOR SHOWER
I SCREENED PORCH
J LOUNGE

Second floor

First floor

16 FT

East elevation

North elevation

West elevation

South elevation

TYPOLOGY:
Single Lifted Bar

MODULES:
2 Boxes, Panelized Saddlebag, and Butterfly Roof

MOUNTAIN RETREAT

Kerhonkson, New York
2005

Located on a five-acre rocky outcrop, the Mountain Retreat trades Manhattan skyscrapers and the scuttle of yellow cabs for sweeping views of the Catskill Mountains and hawks gliding on the thermals below. The client, an outdoor sports enthusiast, camped out on the hilltop during the design phase to confirm the best location, angle, and orientation for his new escape. The modified Single Bar typology is a combination of the Beach House and Suburban case studies. The resulting home is a carefully crafted sanctuary woven into its one-of-a-kind surroundings—providing an experience that the client himself likened to living in a tree house.

The finished design references its rough mountaintop setting directly, with angular lines, soaring height, and a blend of warm cedar siding and cool, gray concrete panels sitting partially on concrete piers. Below the great room, the piers help define the parking spaces for an uncluttered entry and carport. In order to insert the pylons, a well, and a septic tank, the rocky terrain of the immediate site had to be blasted. Rather than discarding the remnants, we scattered the rocks around the site, using them for outdoor seating and pathways, further emphasizing the integration of the house into its natural landscape.

Rainwater channeled from the butterfly roof cascades onto some of these thoughtfully placed boulders that surround the suite of guest rooms on the ground floor. The roof also gives the great room and master bedroom a tall, sloped ceiling that lets in light from above. A panelized saddlebag on the North elevation contains the stair, mechanical equipment, and built-in cabinets, and determines the width of the elevated cedar deck. The deck, perched in the treetops above, wraps around three sides of the great room—providing distant views and offering access to a full day's sunshine, while allowing the entire room to be opened to the outdoors.

The communal space is
elevated upon concrete
piers.

The wraparound deck expands the communal space through a wall of sliding glass doors.

OVERLEAF: Front elevation at dusk.

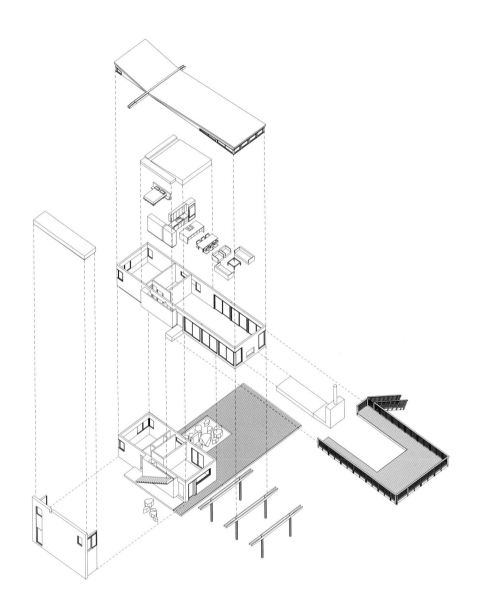

Clerestory windows in the bedroom offer views of the sky, looking above and beyond the nearby woods.

The communal space is conceived in three food-related zones: preparation, consumption, and digestion.

BOTTOM: Kitchen as command center, with the saddlebag beyond, containing built-in cabinets and an interior stair, wrapped with concrete board panels inside and out.

OPPOSITE: Filled with natural light, the communal space expands outward through the sliding glass doors, onto the wraparound deck, and into the surrounding trees.

The elevated living space
offers views of the Catskill
Mountains.

The wraparound deck expands the interior living space.

BOTTOM: The butterfly roof module allows for twelve-foot-high ceilings and clerestory windows.

Second-floor module with the fireplace volume and sliding glass doors along the communal space being set.

BOTTOM: Butterfly roof module with clerestory windows being set.

Second-floor module being set upon concrete piers and the first-floor module.

A   ENTRY
B   KITCHEN
C   DINING
D   LIVING
E   BATH
F   BEDROOM
G   DECK
H   LOUNGE
I   HOT TUB
J   CARPORT

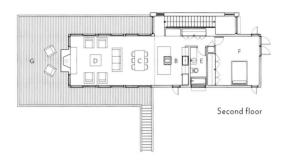

Second floor

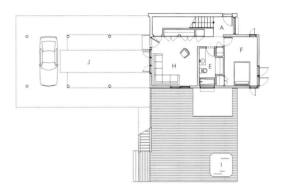

   16 FT

First floor

West elevation

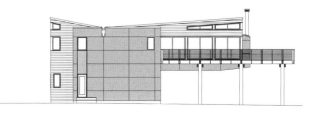

South elevation

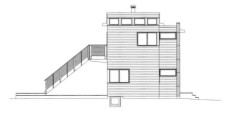

East elevation

North elevation

SWINGLINE

**Wainscott, New York
2007**

Sited on a tree-filled three acres along a busy road, the Swingline is a 4,200-square-foot refuge for a family of six who splits their time between a New York City brownstone and this Hamptons enclave. Designed for relaxing, working, and entertaining extended family and friends all year round, the multigenerational compound contains six bedrooms, a media room, an office, and multiple outdoor spaces, including a pool with an accompanying pool house. As one of the larger structures created with the Modern Modular system, the overall composition is a hybrid of the L, T, and Z typologies.

The main volume of the house is organized as a linear bar positioned parallel with the road. Intended as a wall to create a safe haven for both children and adults, the two-story cedar-clad structure forms an edge defining a landscaped sanctuary to the south protected from traffic. Attached at one end of the long bar is a two-story volume, forming a truncated L to the south with a master suite above and guest suite below. At the other end of the bar sits a detached garage, forming an auto court to the north and establishing the house's overall Z composition. The T typology is represented by two one-story appendages, with one projecting the living space to the south, and another projecting a screened porch to the north.

Upon arrival, family and visitors are welcomed by a large cut into the house framing views of the lush play space and pool house beyond, set deep into the landscape. In addition to suggesting the shape that gave the home its name, this striking passageway creates a threshold both for the property and for the home itself. The main level is dominated by open communal spaces with direct access to exterior spaces. The second floor contains the media room and office to the east of the switchback stair, and to the west, a long corridor with continuous windows facing south becomes a gallery of light leading to a series of private spaces for the family. The combination of typologies and their thoughtful placement on the site allow this sprawling retreat to retain an intimate scale throughout.

Arrival and auto court

Rear elevation at night.

BOTTOM: The entry portal establishes a threshold for both the site and house.

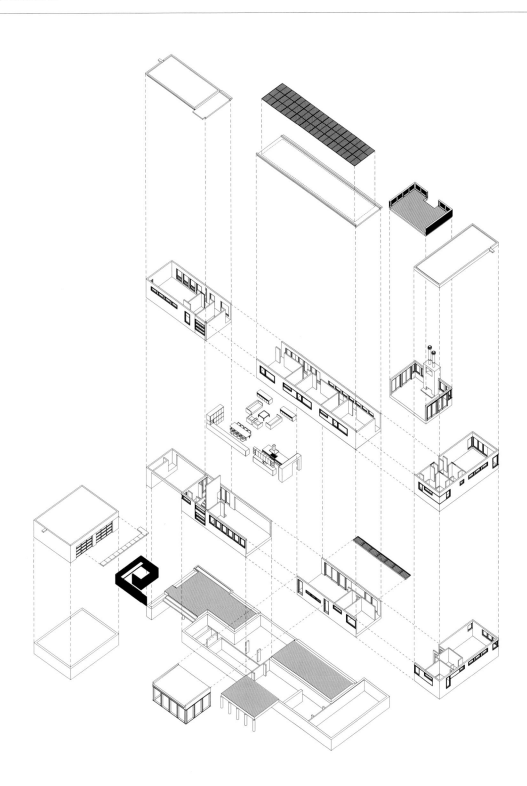

A bluestone path leads to
the detached pool house,
perched upon a concrete
plinth.

Trellis detail.

The pool house sits on axis
with the fireplace volume
and living room module of
the main house beyond.

BOTTOM: Outdoor shower.

Placed parallel to the main
volume of the house, the
large living room module
opens onto flanking decks.

Dining and living spaces are organized along the central fireplace axis.

BOTTOM: The kitchen connects to the screened porch with two glass doors and a horizontal band of counter-height windows.

Second-floor media room and library.

BOTTOM: **Master bedroom.**

The outdoor living room
shares the vertical fireplace
volume with the indoor living
room below.

The wall panel is lowered
into position upon the floor
deck in the factory.

Kitchen module under
inspection in the factory.

BOTTOM: First-floor guest
suite being set.

A   ENTRY
B   KITCHEN
C   DINING
D   LIVING
E   BATH
F   BEDROOM
G   DECK
H   WARDROBE
I   SCREENED PORCH
J   OUTDOOR SHOWER
K   GARAGE
L   MASTER BEDROOM
M   MASTER CLOSET
N   MASTER BATH
O   OFFICE
P   MEDIA ROOM

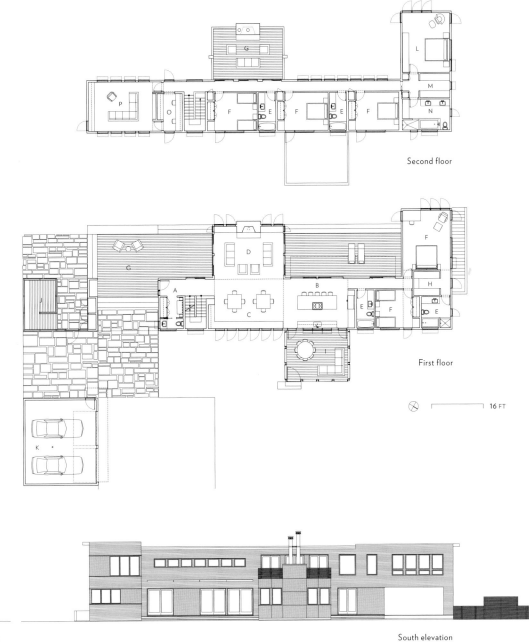

Second floor

First floor

16 FT

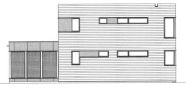

West elevation

South elevation

East elevation

North elevation

BRONX BOX

The Bronx, New York
2008

This urban infill prefab, located at the foot of the Throgs Neck Bridge on Eastchester Bay in the Bronx, was an exciting welcome-home present for the client, a veteran of the war in Iraq. Before her deployment, it was deemed more cost-effective to replace the existing neglected bungalow than to remodel. Given the site's narrow lot, the prefabricated design was able to celebrate the constraints of its particular zoning envelope.

Due to rising waters, a new FEMA flood plane regulation required the house to sit nine feet above grade, towering over neighbors. Additional lot setbacks and height limitations yield a compact footprint while still featuring off-street parking, a small patch of green, and an expansive roof deck with stunning views of the bay and bridge. Additionally, the colors, textures, and materials of the modern design respond to the surrounding fabric, and the house has come to be accepted as another one of the many unique personalities in the eclectic neighborhood.

The Bronx Box is a modified version of the double-decker, Single Bar typology with an additional storage saddlebag, containing built-in cabinets along the length of the house. The compact first level contains an open living, dining, and kitchen area that flows directly onto an elevated deck. Exterior grandstand stairs, which are the full width of the house, serve as a kind of outdoor living room and lead down to a pier that juts out into the bay. The second-floor master suite features its own fireplace and balcony, and a skylight lets natural light into the bathroom. A metal-clad roof bulkhead was carefully sculpted within the zoning restrictions to allow access to the roof deck with 360-degree views of the water and surrounding neighborhood. The Bronx Box demonstrates the efficiency and adaptability of the Modern Modular system within a limited and narrow urban lot.

Street elevation and entry
porch

The living room and infinity deck have views of Eastchester Bay and Throgs Neck Bridge.

BOTTOM: The kitchen's full-height cabinets are contained within the saddlebag.

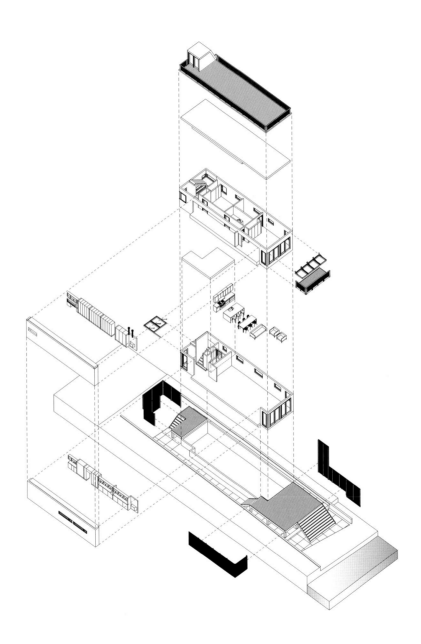

View from the master
bedroom balcony of the
neighboring piers and
Throgs Neck Bridge.

OPPOSITE: The grandstand
stairs connect the house to
the bay.

Second-floor module being
set, as seen from the bay.

BOTTOM: Factory installation
of bamboo flooring and
kitchen cabinets.

Second-floor module
during fabrication, where
the exposed framing
was temporarily used for
shoring during shipping.
Once set, the shoring was
removed, and the panelized
saddlebag was installed.

A   ENTRY
B   KITCHEN
C   DINING
D   LIVING
E   BATH
F   BEDROOM
G   DECK
H   MASTER BEDROOM
I   MASTER BATHROOM

Second floor

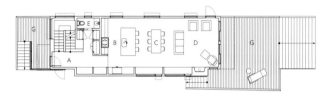

16 FT

First floor

East elevation

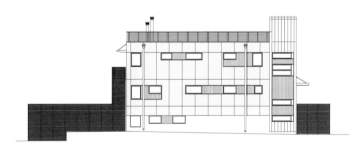

North elevation

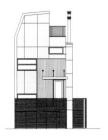

West elevation

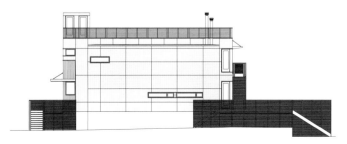

South elevation

TYPOLOGY:

L Series Two-Bar Bridge

MODULES:

6 Boxes and Butterfly Roof

BERKSHIRE HOUSE

West Stockbridge, Massachusetts
2007

Situated three hours north of New York City and two hours west of Boston, the Berkshire Mountains have long been a vacation destination for urban dwellers. This particular escape was designed for a Brooklyn couple and their teenage son for use primarily on the weekends throughout the year. Raised slightly above grade, the house sits in a natural clearing on the edge of a plateau, overlooking a steep drop formed by the Housatonic River.

Leaving the car behind, visitors enter the house up a gently sloping ramp, transitioning to a large outdoor covered space. Designed to accommodate a future screened porch, this entry threshold frames views of the woods, valley, and mountains beyond. The single-story main volume of the home, clad in cement board panels and glass, is placed perpendicularly to the two-story cedar volume. Similar to The Dwell Home, this 2,100-square-foot composition is also a variation of the Two-Bar Bridge in the L Series typology. Both have communal loftlike spaces that are wrapped in floor-to-ceiling glass, surrounded by trees, and flanked by decks. An upper bar of private spaces bridges over the large exterior space, forming a portal to the site.

Whereas The Dwell Home contains a carport under the bridge piece, the Berkshire House includes space for a future screened porch surrounding the house's main entrance. Similar to The Dwell Home though, this home responds to its climate and site with a roof deck, a butterfly roof to collect rainwater, and clerestory windows that face south in the Berkshire's northern climate to maximize solar heat gain. Utilizing the constant temperature of the earth, the Berkshire House is heated and cooled through the use of geothermal energy, increasing the sustainability factor beyond that of The Dwell Home.

Southeast corner

A slightly sloped ipe entry ramp provides a transition from the auto court to the house.

BOTTOM: A covered exterior space frames views through the woods to the Monument Mountain Reserve.

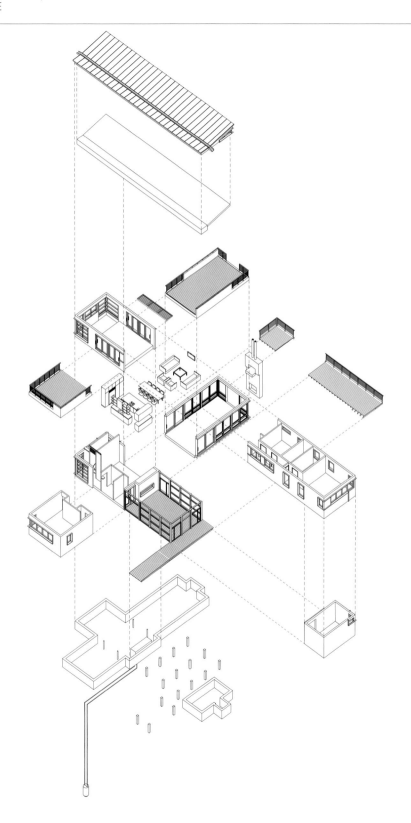

Clad in black steel panels, the fireplace volume is a strong contrast to the woods that surround the living and dining room module.

Organized on axis with the fireplace volume, the kitchen conceals the guest room and bathroom core beyond.

Master bedroom with clerestory windows.

The media room is placed at the top of the stairs. Wrapped in glass, it has access to both north and south roof decks. The lowered ceiling plane compresses the circulation zone and contains the mechanical ductwork above.

OPPOSITE: South roof deck and exterior fireplace.

Butterfly roof module being
lifted from the carrier.

First-floor guest room module
being set.

A ENTRY
B KITCHEN
C DINING
D LIVING
E BATH
F BEDROOM
G DECK
H SCREENED PORCH
I STORAGE
J MEDIA ROOM

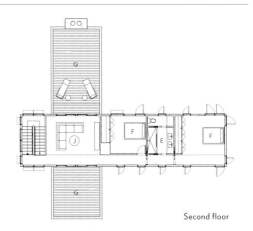

Second floor

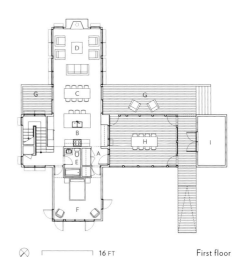

16 FT   First floor

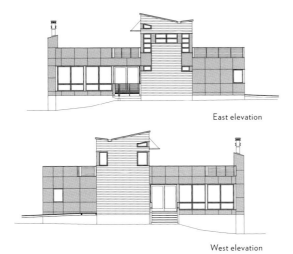

East elevation

West elevation

South elevation

North elevation

HOUSE ON SUNSET RIDGE

Norfolk, Connecticut
2008

Reached via a gently rising spiral drive, this modern prefab home sits perched on a small hill just outside of a town filled with traditional New England architecture. Designed as a country house for a Brooklyn family of four, the house is positioned on axis with a local historical landmark, the fire lookout tower one and a half miles due north on Haystack Mountain. The house is organized in an L configuration, with the kitchen occupying the overlap of the intersecting bars. The first-floor bar contains the public spaces of the home, while the perpendicular upper bar is mostly private. One exception, taking advantage of the L Series typology, is the guest suite, which is set apart on the western end of the first floor and provided with its own private outdoor space and framed meadow views.

Sitting below the upper bar and adjacent to the kitchen, a large screened porch becomes the living and dining space of choice during warm months. The main living area, oriented to align with the distant tower, features a fireplace that is clad in recycled cement board panels. The space is wrapped in glass, maintaining a strong connection to the outdoors even when weather prohibits outdoor living. On the second floor, an exterior deck is located adjacent to the reading room, which doubles as an office. This outdoor area features a green roof and a fireplace, providing a year-round living space with stunning views of the surrounding landscape.

This LEED-certified home is composed of six modules, utilizing the efficiency of off-site factory construction. Like many other homes designed using the Modern Modular system, it employs many innovative and environmentally friendly features, such as bio-based spray foam insulation, a 98 percent energy-efficient boiler, low-flow plumbing fixtures, LED lighting, responsibly harvested ipe and cedar, recycled cement board panels, bamboo floors, radiant floor heating, and a roof wired for solar panels.

Like the traditional homes that occupy the surrounding landscape, this modern home embodies tradition in the making. Embracing an aesthetic of efficiency reflective of today's domesticity, it can be seen from the lookout tower, becoming a landmark of its own within the historical landscape.

The guest suite is accessible by a short walk outside. The exterior cedar cladding of the second-story volume continues as the interior ceiling.

South elevation.

BOTTOM: The screened porch provides summer dining and living space.

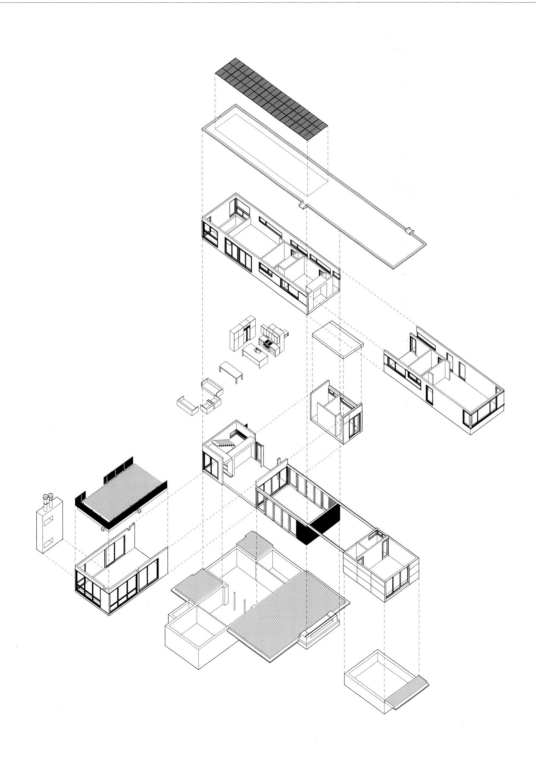

Roof deck, green roof, and exterior fireplace.

BOTTOM: The sliding glass wall opens to connect the guest suite with the exterior.

North facade. The second-floor private module bridges over the screened porch, carport, and guest suite.

The living room frames views
of Haystack Mountain in the
distance.

The interior and exterior of
the fireplace volume is clad
in cement board panels.

The kitchen opens directly
to the screened porch, and
the dining room opens to
an exterior deck.

BOTTOM: The dining and
kitchen areas.

The study, located at the top of the stairs, provides access to the roof deck and is a transition between the first-floor public and second-floor private spaces.

OPPOSITE: Decks are located adjacent to and above the living and dining module.

Master bedroom and
bathroom being set upon the
guest suite below.

BOTTOM: Living and dining
room module being set.

Second-floor module in the
factory.

A   ENTRY
B   KITCHEN
C   DINING
D   LIVING
E   BATH
F   GUEST BEDROOM
G   DECK
H   OUTDOOR SHOWER
I   SCREENED PORCH
J   GREEN ROOF
K   STUDY
L   BEDROOM
M   MASTER BEDROOM
N   MASTER BATH

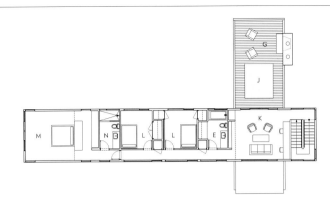

Second floor

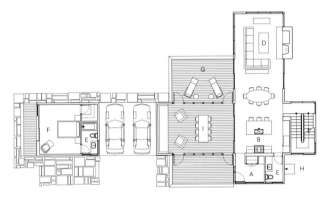

16 FT

First floor

West elevation

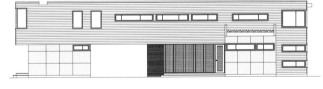

South elevation

East elevation

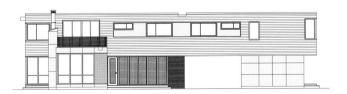

North elevation

TYPOLOGY:
Single Bar

MODULES:
1 Box and Panelized Basement Components

BROWN BAR

Mathias, West Virginia
2008

The Brown Bar is a modern cabin nestled in the rural mountains of scenic West Virginia, two hours west of Washington, D.C. Occupying a very steep slope, the sixteen-foot-wide-by-sixty-four-foot-long Single Bar typology sits perched upon a concrete foundation, terminating the trajectory of a long and winding drive. The home is designed for two uses. One is as a retreat for the client, a family of two schoolteachers and three very young boys living in Washington, D.C. The other is as a rental unit capable of sleeping eight as overnight, weekend, or weekly guests, when not in use by the family.

The main level features a master suite along with the open kitchen, living, and dining areas, including a wood-burning stove—fed by the property's forty-acre supply of seemingly unending biofuel. Capturing sunset views through the trees, the entire west wall of the communal space is floor-to-ceiling operable glass doors and windows. This allows access to the full-length deck that floats in the trees, essentially doubling the communal space during warmer months. A concrete retaining wall creates a forecourt for parking and continues as the basement foundation. The walkout basement on the lower level, finished with polished-concrete floors and radiant heat flooring, includes a media room, an additional guest room, and a bunk room for the kids.

In addition to accommodating family and rental uses, the design attempts to maximize the efficiencies of implementation within the factory, while minimizing the work on-site. Although typical in design and fabrication for all RES4 prefabs, this was unique in that the husband planned to serve as the general contractor himself, tasked with completing all on-site assembly and finishing. To help expedite this process, the house was conceived as one single module, self-contained and complete. The 1,000-square-foot module becomes a 2,000-square-foot home by using the foundation space as a finished walkout basement. All of the lower level's components were shipped from the factory, then assembled on-site and completed by the client himself between semesters.

The Brown Bar, also known as Lost River Modern, is a finely crafted do-it-yourself project, demonstrating the simplicity of the Modern Modular system applied to a rural condition and completed without skilled labor. The result is a serene retreat in a beautiful and natural setting, where only light, sound, and space vie for attention.

Southwest elevation at night

Entry facade. The butterfly
roof captures rainwater and
creates a sloped ceiling
interior.

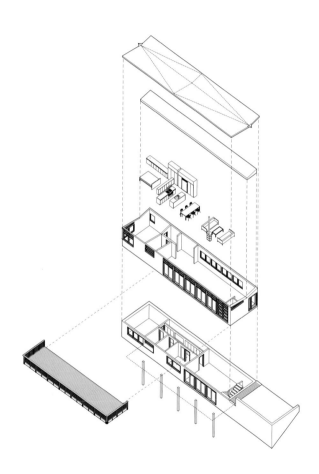

A continuous wall of sliding glass doors and clerestory windows connects the communal space to the exterior.

Dining room and kitchen.
The built-in cabinets along
one edge continue into the
bedroom beyond.

BOTTOM: Master bedroom.

The master bedroom corner
window and clerestory
provide views down the hill
and up into the trees.

Communal space during on-site finishing.

BOTTOM: Installation of cedar siding prior to deck construction. The concrete foundation continues as a retaining wall, forming an auto court above.

The sixteen-by-sixty-four-by-eleven-foot Single Bar module was transported up a steep and winding rural drive.

A   ENTRY
B   KITCHEN
C   DINING
D   LIVING
E   BATH
F   BEDROOM
G   DECK
H   MEDIA ROOM
I   MECHANICAL ROOM

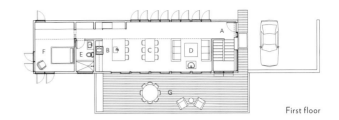

First floor

Lower floor

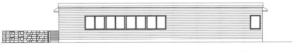

16 FT

South elevation

East elevation

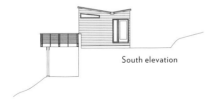

North elevation

West elevation

TYPOLOGY:
L Series Three-Bar Bridge

MODULES:
6 Boxes

HIGH PEAK MEADOW HOUSE

Maplecrest, New York
2009

This two-story L Series typology sits on the highest point of a sloping meadow surrounded by the Catskills Forest Preserve, whose mature trees frame views of nearby Windham High Peak Mountain. Shared by a young family from Manhattan and a grandparent from Connecticut, this second home is composed of two residences integrated as one. A separate mother-in-law suite, containing its own living room, bathroom, and kitchenette, is connected to the main house through a screened porch, which acts as both a separator and connector of the two residences. This centrally located, versatile space allows for individual or communal use throughout the year.

The L Series typology is reflective of the tree line, demarcating the remaining edges of the enclosed meadow. The house's main two-story, cedar-clad volume runs parallel to the road and contains the private spaces. Sitting perpendicularly is a one-story communal volume clad in cement board panels. The composite configuration creates an intimate shaded exterior space complete with an ipe deck floating above the landscape. Smaller in scale, this protected exterior space is analogous to the larger enclosed meadow, which is protected by the trees. And, like the wall of trees surrounding the meadow, the porous layers of the house's porches and glass walls encourage a constant relationship with the naturally layered landscape.

The house is sited on
the highest corner of the
meadow.

The west elevation represents three generations: the master suite sits above the mother-in-law suite, located above the children's playroom.

BOTTOM: The screened porch separates the main living quarters from the mother-in-law suite while connecting the landscape from north to south.

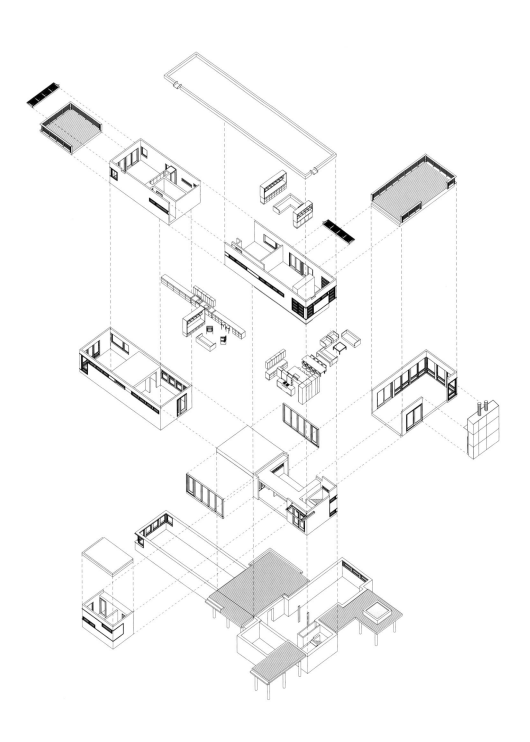

Dining room and kitchen
with a full bath and laundry
room directly behind.

The media room and library have access to the large roof deck. Built-in cabinets conceal the stair beyond.

A black steel-clad volume serves as the fireplace, media wall, and storage unit. Floor-to-ceiling windows frame meadow and mountain views.

BOTTOM: Strand woven bamboo floors wrap around a black steel wall leading down to the main level.

The master bedroom opens onto a private roof deck.

BOTTOM: Built-in cabinets also form the headboard in the master bedroom.

South elevation in summer.

Master bedroom module
being set during summer.

Mother-in-law suite module
under construction in the
factory during late spring.

A   ENTRY
B   KITCHEN
C   DINING
D   LIVING
E   BATH
F   BEDROOM
G   DECK
H   SCREENED PORCH
I   MOTHER-IN-LAW SUITE
J   KITCHENETTE
K   GUEST BEDROOM
L   LAUNDRY
M   MEDIA ROOM
N   MASTER BEDROOM
O   HOT TUB

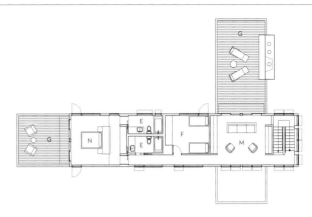

Second floor

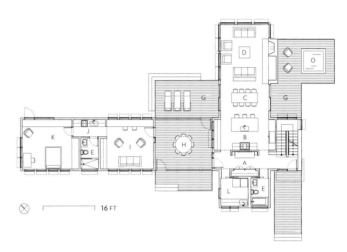

16 FT

First floor

West elevation

East elevation

South elevation

North elevation

CATSKILLS SUBURBAN

Palenville, New York
2009

Located on the edge of a small town in the foothills of the Catskill Mountains, this 2,200-square-foot house occupies a small clearing in the woods. The rectilinear volume sits perpendicular to the end of a long gravel driveway, which continues on as a walking path to a series of hiking trails on Kaaterskill High Peak. Upon arrival, a large Ledgestone wall, quarried locally and stacked by local artisan masons, demarcates the circular auto court while concealing the home's entry. The hand-stacked wall presents a seeming dichotomy with the factory-built house: although built on-site from local materials, its fine craftsmanship relates to the attention to detail that was clearly put into the modular construction behind it. The larger bars were fabricated in two boxes instead of one to better navigate the tight street of the town, through which the house was delivered. The small forty-foot modules

also assist in the heating and cooling of the house, which uses a solar and geothermal energy cogeneration system.

The house sits along the edge of a hiking trail, running north to south along a plateau marked to the west by a thirty-foot rock formation. A two-by-two cedar slat wall provides privacy from the path leading to hiking trails. Designed for a family of four with two young boys who enjoy playing on the lawn and hiking the nearby trails, the house's main level is surrounded by an ipe deck, drawing the interior bamboo floors out onto the exterior lawn. A media room on the second floor serves as a workshop for the video game–designing father, and solid, bold colors throughout reflect the mother's Swedish background and her work in the fashion industry.

North elevation at dusk

Southeast corner.

BOTTOM: The interior and roof deck fireplaces are made of hand-stacked local bluestone.

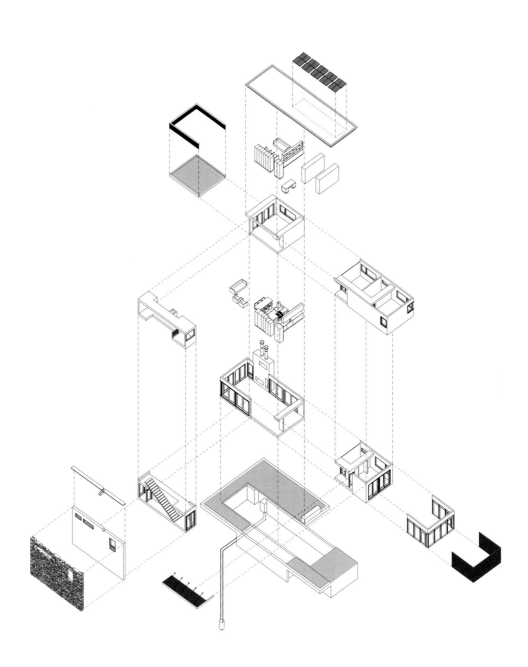

Located on the second floor, the media room has sliding glass doors with access to the roof deck and exterior fireplace.

OPPOSITE: West elevation at dusk.

Master bedroom.

BOTTOM: The cedar ceiling of the guest room extends the space onto a screened porch.

Northeast corner.

The communal space is defined by walls of floor-to-ceiling glass punctuated with a hand-stacked stone fireplace volume.

BOTTOM: The dining room and kitchen spaces open onto the expansive exterior deck.

Kitchen cabinet installation
in the factory.

BOTTOM: Upper-level media
room module being set.

First-floor guest room module
being set upon basement
foundation.

A   ENTRY
B   KITCHEN
C   DINING
D   LIVING
E   BATH
F   BEDROOM
G   DECK
H   SCREENED PORCH
I   OFFICE
J   MEDIA ROOM

Second floor

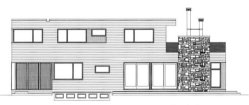

16 FT

First floor

West elevation

South elevation

East elevation

North elevation

TYPOLOGY:
Two-Story Single Bar

MODULES:
4 Boxes and Panelized Saddlebag

LAKE IOSCO HOUSE

Bloomingdale, New Jersey
2009

Similar to many smaller lakes in northern New Jersey, Lake Iosco is sparsely populated, surrounded by only a few homes hidden in the woods along the water's edge. This two-story single bar scheme, designed as a second home for a mother and her son, is positioned as close to the lake as zoning allows. The result is a linear composition oriented from north to south, with complementing sunrise and sunset decks on both sides, and lake views from all rooms.

Large rocks found during the excavation of the basement foundation are used to form a plinth, seen from the approach. A concealed trampoline is set flush with the top of the landscaped plinth. Transitioning from the auto court and up a slight set of stairs, the entry opens to a full-height, freestanding volume with a built-in bench. This bathroom core unit breaks up the otherwise completely open ground floor, demarcating an entry zone and separating a small playroom to the north from a large communal space to the south.

Along the east side is a saddlebag clad in recycled cement board panels that accommodates kitchen cabinets, a black steel fireplace, and media unit. The west side is predominately glass, connecting the space both visually and physically through sliding glass doors to the deck, lawn, and lake—allowing the single mom to easily keep a watchful eye on her young son.

West elevation as seen from
the dam

Master bedroom with custom built-in Baltic birch bed.

BOTTOM: Illuminated by reflections off of the lake, the second floor study is lined with built-in cabinets.

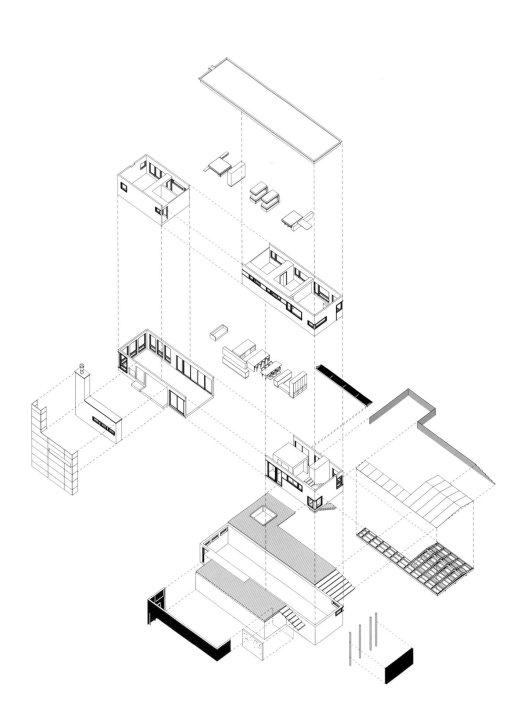

Large rocks found during
excavation form a plinth
concealing a trampoline that
is set flush with the earth.
A polycarbonate carport
extends along the front
facade as an entry canopy,
framing views of the lake
upon arrival.

View from the dining room looking past the kitchen toward the living room. An additional panelized saddlebag to the east accommodates kitchen cabinets and a black steel fireplace and media unit.

Two four-by-eight-foot islands establish circulation along the perimeter, while defining the living, kitchen, and dining zones.

BOTTOM: A bathroom core aligns with the kitchen islands, separating the communal and play spaces, and demarcating the entry.

Northwest corner and lake elevation.

BOTTOM: The dining room sliding glass doors connect the front meadow and morning deck with the rear, lake afternoon deck.

OPPOSITE: The entry steps are concealed by a concrete wall cast with acrylic cylinders and backlit by a motion activated light.

Construction of cedar siding, furring for cement board panels, and deck framing in progress.

First-floor module containing stair, playroom, bathroom core, and entry being set.

BOTTOM: The final cladding installation on-site.

A   ENTRY
B   KITCHEN
C   DINING
D   LIVING
E   BATH
F   BEDROOM
G   DECK
H   PLAY ROOM
I   CARPORT
J   STUDY
K   MASTER BEDROOM
L   HOT TUB

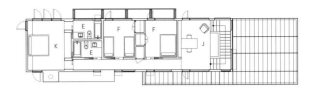

Second floor

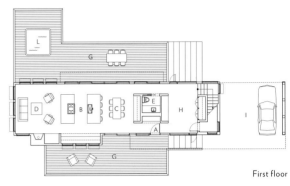

First floor

16 FT

North elevation

West elevation

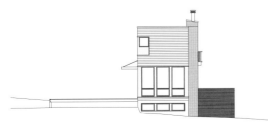

South elevation

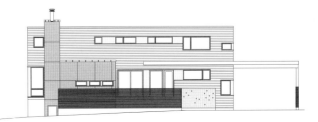

East elevation

TYPOLOGY:
Single Bar

MODULES:
1 Box

CONNECTICUT POOL HOUSE

Sharon, Connecticut
2011

The Connecticut Pool House represents the most elemental typology of the Modern Modular system, the Single Bar series. Located in a natural clearing within a wooded hillside of northwestern Connecticut, this "watering hole" is a welcome reprieve from the clients' hectic urban life. Though small enough to have been delivered on the back of a truck, the sixteen-by-fifty-two-foot module was designed to welcome as many guests as are willing to make the trek from the city. And, given that the clients work in the food and entertainment business, it's no small number of friends and family members that often visit.

Essentially, this simple module acts as a freestanding urban loft with open zones of use. With the pool alongside, the Single Bar typology utilized is closely related to another of the modular typologies, the two-bar slip, except here the second module is replaced by the pool. Inside, between the open living and sleeping areas on either end of the module, sits a recycled black-steel core that contains the service areas and a fireplace. Floating in the loft, this volume is filled with natural light from a skylight above and frosted glass pocket doors.

The house is heated and cooled passively through the expansive wall of sliding glass doors on the south side and the continuous row of operable windows on the north. The roof is designed to accommodate solar hot water panels, to heat not only the pool, but also the house itself via radiant heat tubing beneath the bamboo flooring. In the warmer months, as breezes blow over the pool, water evaporates and cools the air as it comes through the open doors, into the living space, and out the clerestory windows running along the back wall. Although primarily designed for use in the summer, this pool house is sustainably equipped for all seasons.

The house is cooled via evaporative cooling and natural ventilation as breezes blow over the pool and through the house.

A two-by-two cedar construction is used for the entry gate, the barbecue screen wall, and the brise soleil to shield the sliding glass doors from direct sunlight.

BOTTOM: The reflectivity of the glass and water transitions to transparency as day turns to night.

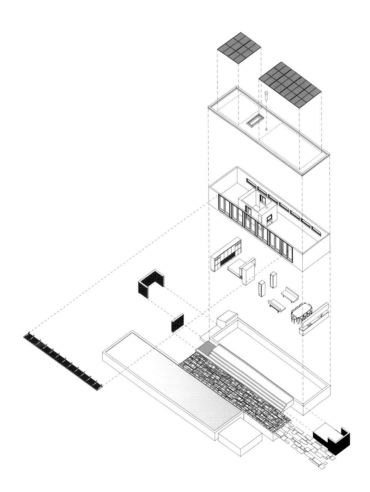

The bluestone terrace
mediates steps leading up
into the house and down into
the pool.

The living room is separated from the bedroom by a black-steel core containing the bathroom with skylight, laundry, storage, and fireplace.

BOTTOM: The custom built-in Baltic birch bed is carved into one end of the black-steel core volume.

The custom Baltic birch four-by-eight-foot table is thirty-six inches high, serving as both table and island.

The sixteen-by-fifty-two-foot module being set.

A   KITCHEN
B   DINING
C   LIVING
D   BATH
E   BEDROOM
F   DECK
G   OUTDOOR SHOWER
H   PATIO
I   POOL

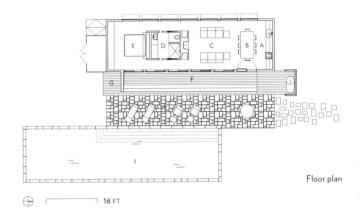

Floor plan

16 FT

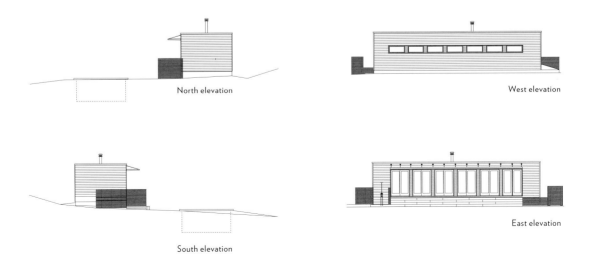

North elevation

West elevation

South elevation

East elevation

FISHERS ISLAND HOUSE

**Fishers Island, New York
2012**

Located off the coast of Connecticut and Rhode Island, yet occupying a body of water in the state of New York, Fishers Island is accessible only by ferry. While during the summer months the island's population swells to over three thousand, year-round residents total only about three hundred. Delivery of daily supplies and materials is therefore limited. Contractors live on the mainland, creating short workdays due to the commute, thereby causing construction of a new home to take longer and effectively cost more. Leveraging off-site construction, shipping volumetric prefabricated modules—complete with plumbing, electrical, and finishes—makes for a much more cost-effective method of building on the island. The boxes were designed specifically not only for the client and site, but also to fit on the standard ferry.

The client, a family of four with two recent college graduates, has extended family that also lives on the island. This house is designed to accommodate and entertain them all for generations to come. Often called "the ark" by locals, the house is composed of eight Lego-like boxes sitting on a panelized concrete foundation that was also prefabricated. Integrated into the sloping landscape, the long and linear vessel is organized by public and private uses. The main level contains communal living spaces that span three parallel boxes, while the second floor contains the immediate family's private spaces. The east wing contains guest rooms and a stair down to a large bunk room below for future grandkids. As the main gathering and entertaining area, the roof becomes another level of living space, essentially an outdoor room, partially covered and equipped with a kitchen, seating, and an outdoor fireplace.

All of the structure's horizontal surfaces are utilized for roof decks, green areas, or solar panels. Hot water generated by the sun keeps the house warm via the radiant floor heating system during colder months.

An evening of entertaining family and friends starts with drinks on the roof deck, then continues downstairs to prepare and consume dinner on the main level. The exterior stair accessed from the parking court in the rear is convenient for guests to join the party upon arrival.

A gently sloping drive
continues through the house,
leading to an auto court and
garage to the north.

North elevation at dusk

BOTTOM: Entry

OVERLEAF: Southeast corner at dusk

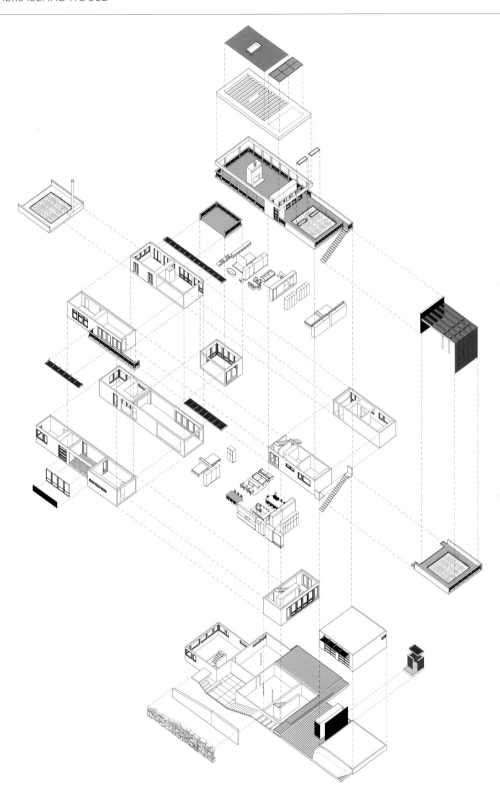

Northeast corner.

BOTTOM: **Supporting solar hot water panels above, the stair bulkhead provides internal access to the upper level roof deck. Glowing skylights surrounded by natural grasses allow natural light into the bathrooms below.**

Screened porch with views of the north meadow.

The upper-level roof deck is equipped with an outdoor fireplace, kitchen, dumbwaiter, and commanding views of the Long Island Sound.

BOTTOM: The exterior stair leads from the auto court to the garage roof deck and upper decks.

The living room faces south toward the Long Island Sound.

BOTTOM: Dining room with living room beyond.

OPPOSITE: The communal space containing the kitchen, dining, and living spaces is created by three overlapping modules placed side by side.

Media room

BOTTOM: **Dining room and kitchen**

Master bathroom and
bedroom suite

BOTTOM: Dining room

One of eight modules being fabricated off site in the factory.

BELOW: The first-floor module containing guest bedroom, stair, screened porch, and kitchen being set upon the prefabricated foundation wall system.

BOTTOM: One of the second-floor bedroom and bathroom modules being set.

A ENTRY
B KITCHEN
C DINING
D LIVING
E SCREENED PORCH
F BATH
G BEDROOM
H DECK
I OUTDOOR SHOWER
J GARAGE
K MEDIA ROOM
L MASTER BEDROOM
M MASTER BATHROOM
N GREEN ROOF

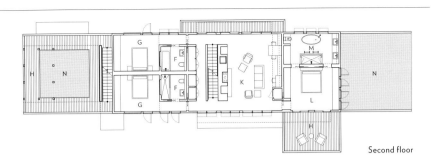

Second floor

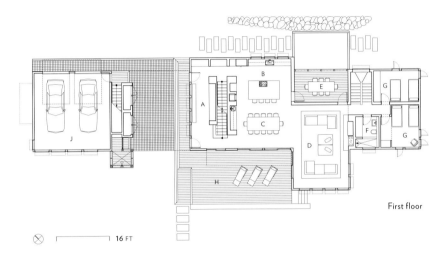

First floor

16 FT

West elevation

North elevation

East elevation

South elevation

TYPOLOGY:
Two-Story Double-Wide

MODULES:
4 Boxes

DUNE ROAD BEACH HOUSE

East Quogue, New York
2012

The eastern end of Long Island has a rich history of architect-designed beach houses. This home is located off the renowned Dune Road, where most houses are twice its size (many are five or even ten times as big). The site is located on a long, thin barrier reef, connected back to the mainland by bridge. This setting provides the house with views not only of the ocean immediately to the south, but also of the bay and marshland to the north. Analogous to the narrow barrier reef, the home's interior is organized as a linear composition, with service spaces, such as bathrooms, kitchen, mechanical rooms, and vertical circulation, to the north, and open living and sleeping areas to the south. The client is a young family living in a large apartment in downtown Manhattan. Unlike most second homes owned by city dwellers, this house is actually smaller than their apartment. Accordingly, time spent here is more akin to camping on the beach than escaping to a rural fortress.

The house sits at the end of a long drive and the main entry is reached over a long ramp that bridges the naturally duned landscape. The lot is one of the last remaining of its kind, with the house sited right beside the ocean, riding the crest of the dune. The site is grandfathered in to pass the typical allowable building line, since the new construction replaced a dilapidated beach bungalow, which was falling apart due to the crashing waves. The foundation is a series of forty-five-foot-long wood piers, resembling telephone poles, driven deep into the sand, upon which the two lower floor boxes are set. Zoning and allowable square footage requirements determined not only the home's placement, but also its length, width, and height. In addition to the home's hurricane-rated structure and windows, the dune was rebuilt per environmental standards for protection from any potential damage from the ocean.

The floor-to-ceiling glass wall in the communal space has the effect of sitting on the beach while retaining all the comforts of home. The second level has four bedrooms, including a bunk room, and interior stairs leading to a roof deck with a fireplace, a hot tub, a space for morning yoga, and views up and down the beach, high above the surrounding houses.

Southwest corner from
beach

North elevation as seen
from Dune Road

OVERLEAF: South elevation
at dusk

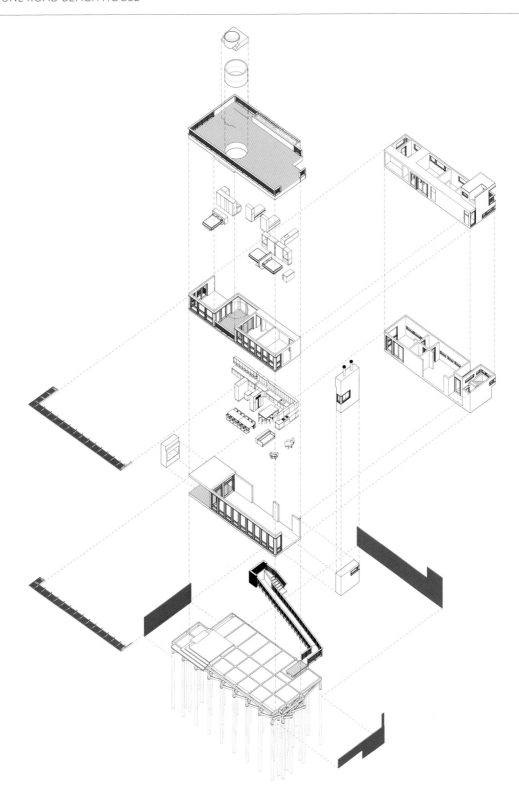

Oculus deck

BOTTOM: Bunk room with oculus deck and ocean beyond

Master bedroom   Guest bedroom   BOTTOM: Master bathroom

The upper-level roof deck is an outdoor living room with views of the Atlantic Ocean to the South and Shinnecock Bay to the North.

OPPOSITE: The oculus deck serves as an oversized sun dial.

A wall of floor-to-ceiling
glass offers expansive views
of the ocean. The long and
linear nature of the coastline
is captured within the
proportions of the communal
space.

Living room and view of
Atlantic Ocean upon entry.

BOTTOM: Kitchen cabinets
and horizontal slot windows
frame views of the bay to the
north.

Second-floor module
containing guest bedrooms,
oculus deck, and master
bedroom being set as seen
from neighboring house.

BOTTOM: Detail of second-
floor module being set.

The modules during off-site
factory construction.

A   ENTRY
B   KITCHEN
C   DINING
D   LIVING
E   BATH
F   OFFICE
G   DECK
H   BEDROOM
I   MASTER BEDROOM
J   MASTER BATH
K   HOT TUB

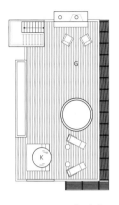

Roof plan

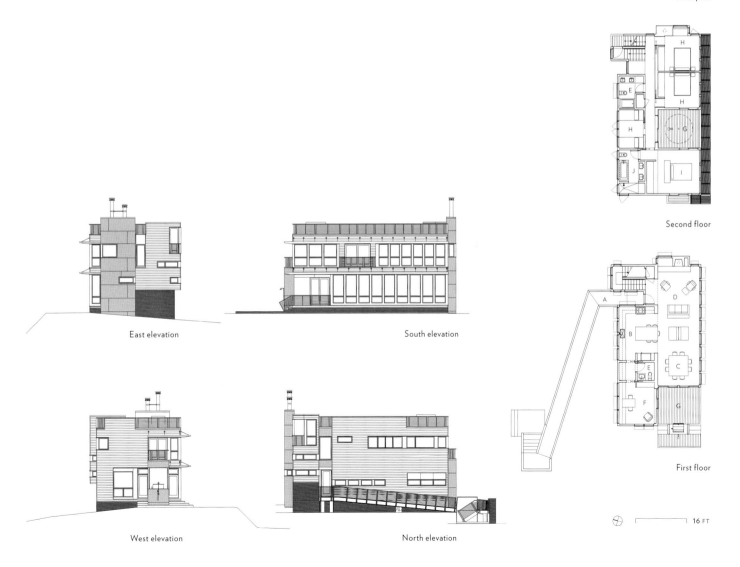

East elevation

South elevation

West elevation

North elevation

Second floor

First floor

16 FT

PREFAB SYSTEMS

Resolution: 4 Architecture has designed over 120 prefab homes based on the Modern Modular, in locations ranging from Maine to Hawaii. Shown here are a variety of modular, panelized, and hybrid delivery methods.

BLUE RIDGE MOUNTAIN HOUSE
Asheville, NC

2006

L Series

JERSEY SHORE HOUSE
Long Branch, NJ

2007

Hybrid L Series/Double-Wide

SILVERLAKE TWINS
Los Angeles, CA

2007

Single Bar

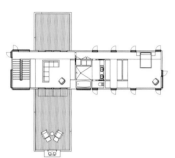

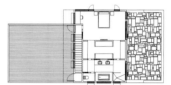

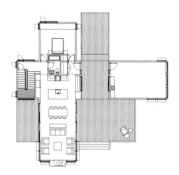

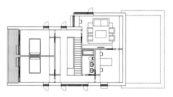

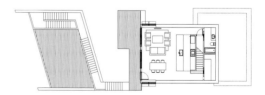

BEVERLY HILLS HOUSE
Beverly Hills, CA
2006
Hybrid Z Series, Courtyard

FIT HOUSE AT SAGAPONAC
Sagaponac, NY
2008
Z Series

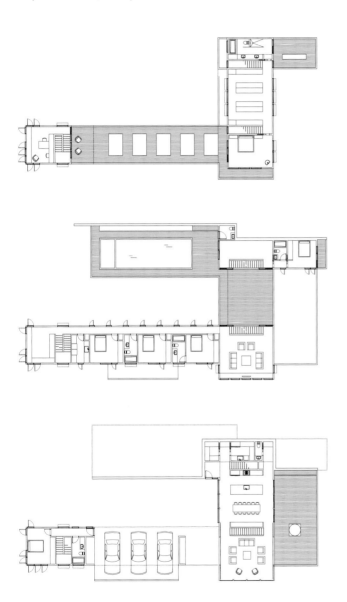

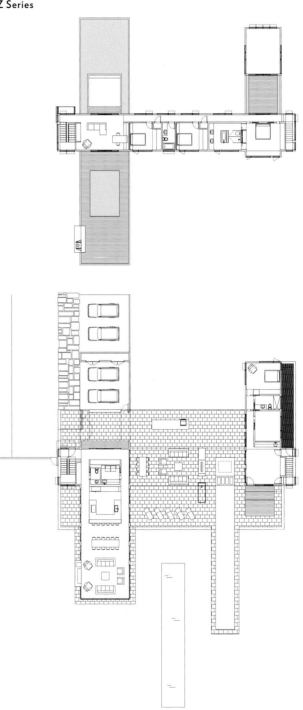

ARTIST RETREAT
Watermill, NY

2006

Hybrid L Series/T Series

EAST VILLAGE HOUSING
New York, NY

2005

Double-Wide

LOS GATOS
Los Gatos, CA

2008

Courtyard Series

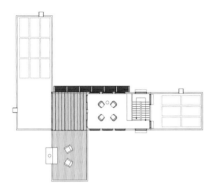

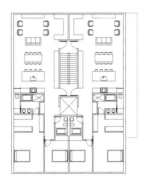

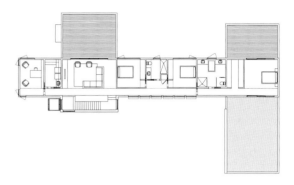

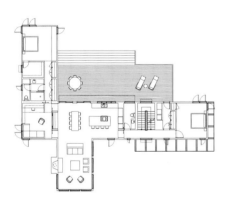

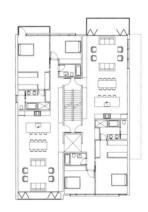

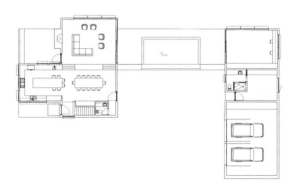

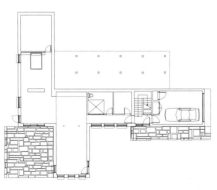

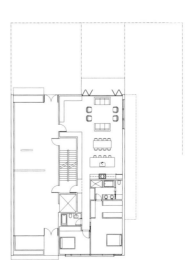

COUNTRY RETREAT
The Plains, VA
2006
L Series

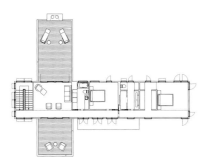

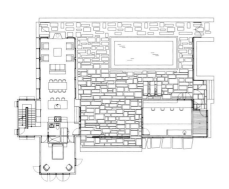

OLIVE BRIDGE HOUSE
Olive, NY
2012
L Series

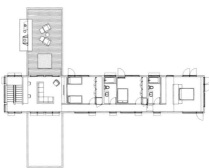

HAWK RIDGE RESIDENCE
Ellenville, NY
2005
Z Series

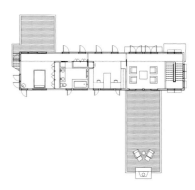

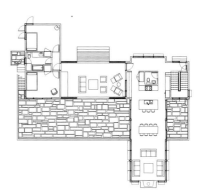

BEAR RUN
Shokan, NY
2008
Triple-Wide

SUMMER RETREAT
East Hampton, NY

2005

Z Series

MANHATTAN BEACH HOUSE
Brooklyn, NY

2009

Hybrid Triple-Wide/L Series

HARMONY HILL HOUSE
East Meredith, NY

2006

Hybrid L Series/T Series

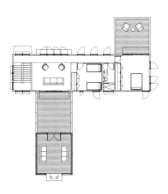

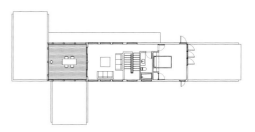

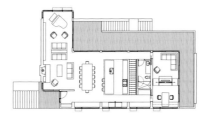

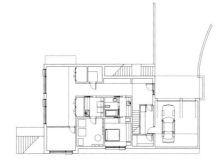

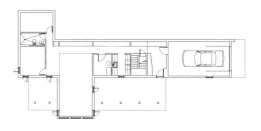

SILVER BOX
Redding, CT
2005
Single Bar

LIDO BEACH HOUSE
Lido Beach, NY
2008
Hybrid Double-Wide/Courtyard Series

HAWAII DWELLING
Maui, HI
2007
L Series

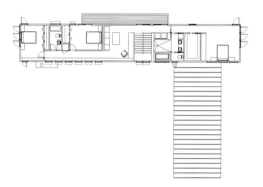

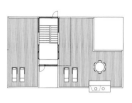

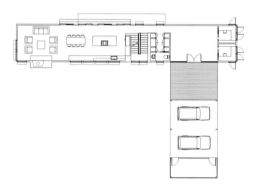

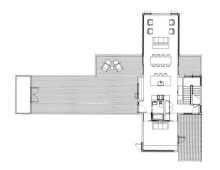

HARMONY HILL CABINS
East Meredith, NY
2004
Single Bar

EDGE HOUSE
Jewett, NY
2012
Double-Wide

CENTER PARCS MOSELLE
Paris, France
2006
Z Series

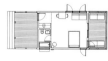

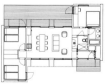

LONG BEACH COTTAGE
Long Beach, NY
2012
Single Bar

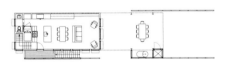

SUBURBAN VILLA
Bethesda, MD
2012
Double-Wide

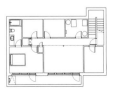

DUNE ACRES
Chesterton, IN
2006
Single Bar

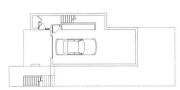

VERMONT CABIN
Jamaica, VT
2009
Hybrid Triple-Wide/L Series

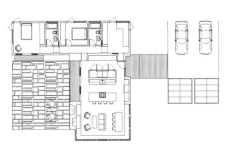

PALOMAR HOUSE IN THE HILLS
San Diego, CA
2006
T Series

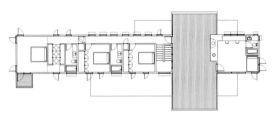

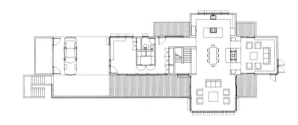

WISCONSIN CABIN
Baileys Harbor, WI
2011
Double-Wide

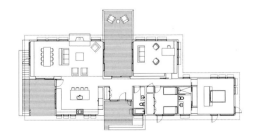

LEIGHTON MAINE RETREAT

Brooklin, ME

2006

L Series

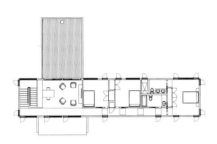

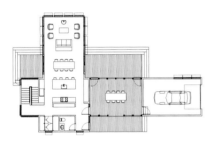

HUDSON VALLEY HOUSE

Stanfordville, NY

2006

Double-Wide

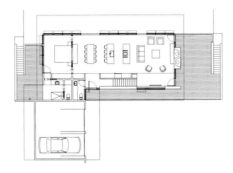

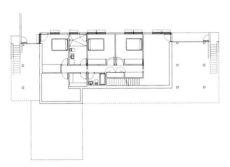

PECONIC BAY HOUSE

Shinnecock Hills, NY

2007

Single Bar

ATLANTIC BEACH HOUSE

Atlantic Beach, NY

2006

Double-Wide

LITTLE FLOWER

San Diego, CA

2007

Double-Wide

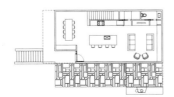

CATSKILLS ENCHANTED COTTAGE

Marbletown, NY

2008

Double-Wide

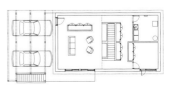

DUNE HOUSE
Bridgman, MI

2006

Double-Wide

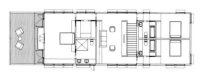

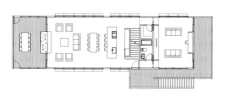

BROWN BOX
Saugerties, NY

2006

Double-Wide

THE WHITE HOUSE
Columbia County, NY

2006

Triple-Wide

HOUSE ON MARTHA'S VINEYARD
Chilmark, MA

2005

T Series

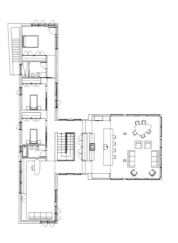

SANDY LAKE HOUSE
Ashland, NE

2006

Single Bar

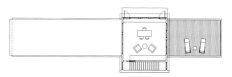

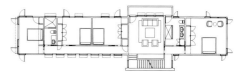

POCONO SUBURBAN
Poconos, PA

2007

Single Bar

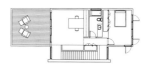

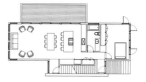

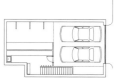

VENICE BEACH HOUSE
Venice, CA
2006
Courtyard Series

HOUSE ON CHESAPEAKE BAY
Annapolis, MD
2004
Z Series

BLACK RIVER HOUSE
Benton Harbor, MI
2007
Z Series

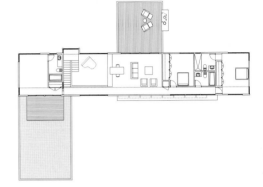

BERKSHIRE CABIN
New Marlborough, MA
2005
Triple-Wide

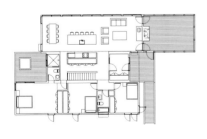

SUNDANCE FILM HOUSE
Park City, UT
2006
Double-Wide

SAGAPONAC LOT 29

Sagaponac, NY

2011

Hybrid Triple-Wide/T Series

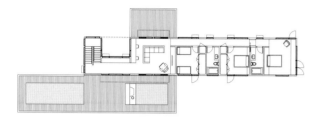

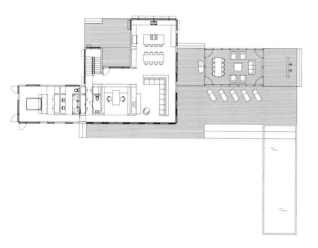

LOW-RISE HIGH-DENSITY HOUSING

Boulder, CO

2007

Varies: Hybrid Z Series, Courtyard, L Series, and Single Bar

HILLSIDE URBAN TOWNHOUSES

Los Angeles, CA

2006

Varies

ACKNOWLEDGMENTS

The manifestation of architecture is only possible with a team. Since starting the practice in 1990, our intention has been to produce a body of work with resolve, and the Modern Modular has developed out of this mentality.

Over the last twenty years, we have been very fortunate to have a group of exceptionally talented people in the office. It is their commitment, dedication, and enthusiasm upon which our practice thrives. We would especially like to thank the following, without whom the work in this book would not have been possible: Dave Freeland, Michael MacDonald, John Kim, Craig Kim, Shawn Brown, Jeff Straesser, Jerome Engelking, Catarina Ferreira, Brian Thomas, Richard Kim, Jacob Moore, Matt Clarke, Michael Hargens, Diane Pham, Se Jung, Kara Yamagami, Kyle Day, Kristen Mason, Brendan Miller, Paul Coughlin, Amir Mikhaeil, Justin Barnes, Patty Clayton, Andrew Herbert, and Terrence Seah. These incredibly hands-on individuals have drawn, modeled, coordinated (in office, factory, and on-site), photographed, written about, slept in, and even built portions of the projects, and we will always be indebted for their contributions.

As with all built work, none of the ideas represented here would have been realized without our clients. We are grateful to all of our past and current clients, for it is an honor to be asked to design anything and a true privilege to design someone's personal space. We are especially thankful to Nathan Wieler and Ingrid Tung, owners of The Dwell Home, our first prefabricated project.

Fabricating a modern home is not standard practice for the modular industry. We thank Elliot Fabri and Carolina Building Solutions for building our first Modern Modular and helping us to pioneer a new standard. George Clark and Bob Nipple of Apex, Roger Lyons of Penn Lyon, Dick Rowe of Integrity Building Systems, and Dave Endy of Stratford Homes were also among the first manufacturers to help us realize our vision. We give special thanks to Patrick Gilrane and Michael Harris of Empyrean, with whom we built panelized homes from Maine to Hawaii. Most importantly, we are grateful to Simplex Industries. Under the leadership of Pat Fricchione, Dave Boniello, and Dave Mertz, Simplex has worked with us to develop our best work. We thank Jason Drouse for his day-to-day management and Paul Walker for his impeccable coordination of fabrication drawings. Over one hundred hands touch each box before it leaves the factory, and we thank everyone at Simplex for their efforts.

Typically, 80 percent of a modular home is fabricated off site. Yet without the skills and watchful eye of the on-site general contractor to assemble and finish them, the modules would remain uninhabitable boxes. We would like to thank all of our general contractors for their contributions, specifically Scott Reeves, Jim Nelson, and Gasper Teresi for their craft and attention to detail. We thank Joe Tortorella of Robert Sillman Associates for the structural engineering of our first six projects, and Lynn Walshaw for her many contributions since. Lynn's structural engineering has allowed our homes to withstand even the wrath of Hurricane Sandy. We are also thankful to Bob Yaciuk; his highly efficient high-velocity mechanical system allows for installation in the factory. In terms of engineering and overall modular knowledge, we are most thankful to Greg Sloditskie—our secret weapon—for he has helped us navigate the nuances of a modular industry that is leery of the architect.

And without *Dwell*, the resurgence of the prefab movement might not exist at all. We are indebted to everyone there (and their readers) for featuring our work and continuing to shine a bright light on the world of prefab. We want to thank Michela O'Conner Abrams, Shelly Tatum Kieran, Sam Grawe, and most recently Amanda Dameron. Most significantly we want to thank Allison Arieff, who in addition to writing the foreword to this book, literally wrote the book on prefab with Byran Burkhart. Thanks to them, we were inspired to launch a website featuring our research of the Modern Modular. We have been fortunate to develop relationships with others participating in this prefab space. We'd like to acknowledge the camaraderie and inspiration of Charlie Lazor, Michelle Kaufmann, Rocio Romero, Joel Turkel, and Geoff Warner. And a special recognition of Michael Sylvester, whose knowledge and insight helped us frame our work in terms of architecture versus product.

We are grateful to all of the editors and writers who have featured our work, including but not limited to Lloyd Adler, Dan Akst, Fred Bernstein, Justin Davidson, Dianne Daniel,

William Lamb, and Sara Hart. In addition to *Dwell*, we thank the publications, both print and digital, that have recognized our projects and exposed our work to potential clients: newspapers such as the *Wall Street Journal*, the *New York Times*, the *Boston Globe*, the *Washington Post*, the *Chicago Tribune*, *New York Newsday*, *Los Angeles Times*; journals such as *Architecture*, *Architectural Record*, *Architectural Review*, *Domus*, *LARCA*, *Interni*, *Residential Architect*; popular magazines such as *Time*, *Newsweek*, *Wired*, *Food & Wine*, *Metropolitan Home*, and *House & Garden*; and numerous books published by Taschen, Wiley, W. W. Norton, Harpers Collins, Designzens, RIHAN, Hauser, Universe, DAAB, Braun, Monsa, and additional international publishers. We are also grateful and honored that the Modern Modular has been featured on television networks, including CNN, HGTV, the Travel Channel, DIY, *CBS Morning News*, and *Nightline*.

For the specific efforts of compiling this book, we are forever grateful to Patty Clayton, Craig Kim, and Brendan Miller. We thank our editors at Princeton Architectural Press— Megan Carey, Jacob Moore, and Meredith Baber. We appreciate Jan Haux's rigorous design, and we are grateful to everyone at PAP for their patience.

The ongoing investigation of our prefab efforts has been supported by the following academic institutions, and we thank them for inviting us to lecture, teach, present, exhibit, critique, and debate our work with others preoccupied with methods of prefabrication:

Harvard University, Columbia University, University of Minnesota, Yale University, University of Pennsylvania, University of Kentucky, City College of New York, Virginia Tech, Eastern Carolina University, Tecnólogico de Monterrey in Mexico City, Arizona State University, University of Colorado at Boulder, Massachusetts Institute of Technology, University of Virginia, Northeastern University, Southern Polytechnic State University, University of Florida, Parsons New School for Design, University of Las Vegas, Pratt Institute, Rensselaer Polytechnic Institute, Rutgers University, and Stanford University. We want to thank the following professional and cultural institutions for the various awards, lectures, symposiums, conferences, and exhibitions featuring the Modern Modular: the Museum of Modern Art, *Massive Change* international exhibition, the National Building Museum, Heckscher Museum, Hammer Museum, Walker Art Center, Vancouver Art Gallery, Virginia Center for Architecture, Nevada Museum of Art, Yale Art and Architecture Gallery, the Museum of Contemporary Art Los Angeles, the Boston Society of Architects, AIA New York, AIA Connecticut, AIA Chesapeake Bay, the Chicago Athenaeum, AIA Minnesota, AIA New England, AIA New Jersey, Virginia Society AIA, AIA South Carolina, AIA San Francisco, Black Rock Design Institute, AIA North Carolina, and the Architectural League of New York.

We appreciate our professors, who continue to have a lasting impact on our thinking about the production of architecture: Bobby Vuyosevich on how to diagram a plan and Doug Graf on how to diagram an idea; Robert Livesey instilled a constant search for clarity and Jeff Kipnis instilled a constant search for ambiguity; George Ranalli exposed the essence of utility; Charles Gwathmey taught the importance of the edit and the value of reduction, and to always attempt to articulate and not merely accommodate; and Peter Eisenman taught to first and foremost establish your constraints, and only then can you use your discretion within them, which develops from observation and experimentation. Eisenman also stressed to always be looking, analyzing, speculating, and ultimately proposing reinterpretations. Because architecture is a process and not a product, we must constantly put forth an effort to evolve the discipline—an effort that the Modern Modular embodies.

And of course, we'd like to give the ultimate thanks to our families. We appreciate Nancy, Claudia, Rachel, Christina, Suzanne, Sarah, Daniel, David, Jim, and Rosemary for supporting us in what we love to do.

This book is dedicated to all of you who have at one time or another pursued the Holy Grail of modernism: to those of you who have helped make it happen for us so far and especially to those of you who will do so in the future.

PROJECT CREDITS

THE DWELL HOME

ARCHITECTS:
Joseph Tanney, Robert Luntz
PROJECT ARCHITECT:
Michael MacDonald
PROJECT TEAM:
Shawn Brown, Jerome Engelking, Catarina Ferreira, Craig Kim, John Kim, Jeff Straesser
MANUFACTURER:
Carolina Building Solutions
CONTRACTOR:
Mount Vernon Homes
PHOTOGRAPHERS:
Roger Davies, Jerry Markatos, Wes Milholen, RES4

CAPE HOUSE

ARCHITECTS:
Joseph Tanney, Robert Luntz
PROJECT ARCHITECTS:
Craig Kim, John Kim
PROJECT TEAM:
Michael Hargens, Richard Kim, Brian Thomas
MANUFACTURER:
Simplex Industries
ENGINEERS:
Greg Sloditskie; Lynne Walshaw, P.E.
CONTRACTOR:
Twine Field Custom Builders
PHOTOGRAPHERS:
Joshua McHugh, RES4

MOUNTAIN RETREAT

ARCHITECTS:
Joseph Tanney, Robert Luntz
PROJECT ARCHITECT:
John Kim

PROJECT TEAM:
Craig Kim, Richard Kim, Jacob Moore
MANUFACTURER:
Apex Homes
ENGINEERS:
Robert Silman Associates, Greg Sloditskie
CONTRACTOR:
JH Construction
PHOTOGRAPHERS:
Floto & Warner, RES4

SWINGLINE

ARCHITECTS:
Joseph Tanney, Robert Luntz
PROJECT ARCHITECTS:
Paul Coughlin, Jerome Engelking
PROJECT TEAM:
Michael Hargens, Se Jung, Richard Kim
MANUFACTURER:
Simplex Industries
ENGINEERS:
Greg Sloditskie; Lynne Walshaw, P.E.; Bob Yaciuk
LANDSCAPE ARCHITECT:
Robin Key Landscape Design
LANDSCAPE CONTRACTOR:
April Gonzales
CONTRACTOR:
JRL Construction
PHOTOGRAPHERS:
Miko Almaleh, Francine Fleischer, RES4

BRONX BOX

ARCHITECTS:
Joseph Tanney, Robert Luntz

PROJECT ARCHITECTS:
Craig Kim, John Kim
MANUFACTURER:
Simplex Industries
ENGINEERS:
Greg Sloditskie, Lynne Walshaw, P.E., Bob Yaciuk
CONTRACTOR:
Northbrook Contracting
PHOTOGRAPHERS:
Laurie Lambrecht, RES4

BERKSHIRE HOUSE

ARCHITECTS:
Joseph Tanney, Robert Luntz
PROJECT ARCHITECTS:
Shawn Brown, Brian Thomas
PROJECT TEAM:
John Kim, Michael MacDonald, Brendan Miller
MANUFACTURER:
Simplex Industries
ENGINEERS:
Greg Sloditskie; Lynne Walshaw, P.E.
CONTRACTOR:
Small Building Company
PHOTOGRAPHER:
RES4

HOUSE ON SUNSET RIDGE

ARCHITECTS:
Joseph Tanney, Robert Luntz
PROJECT ARCHITECT:
Brian Thomas
PROJECT TEAM:
John Kim, Michael MacDonald, Brendan Miller

MANUFACTURER:

Simplex Industries

ENGINEERS:

Greg Sloditskie; Lynne Walshaw, P.E.

LEED CONSULTANT:

Jay Walsh

LANDSCAPE ARCHITECT:

Susannah Drake

CONTRACTOR:

D. Scott Reeves Construction

PHOTOGRAPHER:

RES4

BROWN BAR

ARCHITECTS:

Joseph Tanney, Robert Luntz

PROJECT ARCHITECT:

John Kim

PROJECT TEAM:

Kara Yamagami

MANUFACTURER:

Simplex Industries

ENGINEERS:

Greg Sloditskie; Lynne Walshaw, P.E.

CONTRACTOR:

Chris Brown

PHOTOGRAPHERS:

Chris Brown, Chris Mueller, RES4

HIGH PEAK MEADOW HOUSE

ARCHITECTS:

Joseph Tanney, Robert Luntz

PROJECT ARCHITECT:

Amir Mikhaeil

PROJECT TEAM:

John Kim, Brendan Miller

MANUFACTURER:

Simplex Industries

ENGINEERS:

Greg Sloditskie; Lynne Walshaw, P.E.

CONTRACTOR:

Rick Hutchinson, EcoSmart Homes, Nelson Contracting

PHOTOGRAPHER:

RES4

CATSKILLS SUBURBAN

ARCHITECTS:

Joseph Tanney, Robert Luntz

PROJECT ARCHITECTS:

John Kim, Brian Thomas

PROJECT TEAM:

Patty Clayton, Terrence Seah

MANUFACTURER:

Simplex Industries

ENGINEERS:

Greg Sloditskie; Lynne Walshaw, P.E.

CONTRACTOR:

Nelson Contracting

PHOTOGRAPHER:

RES4

LAKE IOSCO HOUSE

ARCHITECTS:

Joseph Tanney, Robert Luntz

PROJECT ARCHITECT:

Kristen Mason

PROJECT TEAM:

Patty Clayton, Andrew Herbert

MANUFACTURER:

Simplex Industries

ENGINEERS:

Greg Sloditskie; Lynne Walshaw, P.E.; Bob Yaciuk

CONTRACTOR:

D Woodard Builder

PHOTOGRAPHERS:

Steve Hockstein/Harvard Studio, RES4

CONNECTICUT POOL HOUSE

ARCHITECTS:

Joseph Tanney, Robert Luntz

PROJECT ARCHITECT:

Paul Coughlin

PROJECT TEAM:

Patty Clayton

MANUFACTURER:

Simplex Industries

ENGINEERS:

Greg Sloditskie, Mike Tomko

CONTRACTOR:

D. Scott Reeves Construction

PHOTOGRAPHER:

RES4

FISHERS ISLAND HOUSE

ARCHITECTS:

Joseph Tanney, Robert Luntz

PROJECT ARCHITECTS:

Paul Coughlin, Brendan Miller

PROJECT TEAM:

Patty Clayton, Andrew Herbert, Terrence Seah

MANUFACTURER:

Simplex Industries

ENGINEER:

Greg Sloditskie; Lynne Walshaw, P.E.; Bob Yaciuk

LANDSCAPE ARCHITECT:

Reed Hilderbrand Associates

LIGHTING CONSULTANT:

Max von Barnholt

DECORATOR:

David Bentheim

CONTRACTOR:

BD Remodeling & Restoration

PHOTOGRAPHER:

RES4

DUNE ROAD BEACH HOUSE

ARCHITECTS:

Joseph Tanney, Robert Luntz

PROJECT ARCHITECT:

Paul Coughlin

PROJECT TEAM:

Patty Clayton, Andrew Herbert, John Kim, Kristen Mason

MANUFACTURER:

Simplex Industries

ENGINEERS:

Greg Sloditskie; Lynne Walshaw, P.E.; Bob Yaciuk

CONTRACTOR:

Teresi Construction

PHOTOGRAPHER:

RES4